Indian 101

For Tatun and Nani, who first sparked my love of cooking –
a fire that continues to guide me and burn brighter every single day.

Karan Gokani

Indian 101

Real Indian Recipes Made Simple

BLUEBIRD

Contents

Welcome to
INDIAN 101

~~~~~~

While Indian food and ingredients are a lot more prevalent in the West today than they were a couple of decades ago, I still feel that Indian cooking is often oversimplified, bastardized or misunderstood. There is so much more to it than tarka dal and chicken tikka masala; or complicated restaurant-style recipes. Indian cooking can be simple, accessible, varied and fun. The food we eat at home every day is vastly different from that found in most restaurants. I want to introduce (or maybe reintroduce) home cooks to simple Indian recipes that are easy to follow and give you a real flavour of the incredible cuisine of the subcontinent, beyond the usual. This is what *Indian 101* sets out to do.

I'm fast approaching that point in my life where I've lived in the UK as long as I did growing up in India. I've got family, friends and close links to both countries, and strangely refer to both as 'home', in conversation as well as in thought. Living in London has taught me so much about food, cooking and culture across the globe. But food from the Indian subcontinent still remains the food we cook the most at home, and seek at restaurants most frequently. And so, when I began plotting this book, I couldn't think of anything more exciting to write about than the food I grew up eating and that I cook at home all the time.

Take a bowl of Punjabi rajma, a comforting kidney bean stew from North India, pair it with some steamed rice, and you have the ultimate comforting weeknight meal. Or consider a Chettinad chicken curry from the South, packed with flavour, ready to take centre stage at your next dinner party. Parsi eggs on potatoes make for the perfect weekend brunch, while Bengali-inspired baked

mustard fish is an ideal choice for a quick, satisfying lunch. These diverse dishes from the four corners of the country are unmistakably Indian, yet incredibly easy to prepare, with minimal effort and a handful of ingredients. What's best is that they don't need to be eaten as part of a feast and can be enjoyed by themselves, or served simply with rice, rotis, bread or any carb of your choice.

Indian food is not always hot and you don't always need a cupboard full of spices to make a single dish.

Indian 101 isn't a masterclass on Indian cookery, but rather an attempt to give you an easy, digestible taste of the nuances and diversity of Indian food. I want this book to give you a feel for real Indian cooking, while remaining approachable and very achievable – showcasing food that is cooked simply, efficiently and quickly in homes across the nation, every day.

I've tried my best to include something in here for everyone, no matter where you live, your level of proficiency in the kitchen, or your familiarity with India and its food. I hope this collection of recipes gets you as excited about Indian food as I am.

So come join me in the kitchen and let me (re)introduce you to Indian food. This is *Indian 101*.

Indian Regional Food

India is a vast country, and I'm willing to stick my neck out and say its food is more diverse than that which can be found across entire continents (well . . . some at least). Travel just a hundred kilometres in India and you'll probably encounter a different language and people, with new ingredients and dishes to discover. Consequently, I make no claims of knowing everything about or representing food from every one of the twenty-eight States and eight Union Territories of India. In fact, I've missed a majority of them in this book.

The recipes here merely offer a glimpse into the vast and varied world of Indian cuisine, giving you a taste of the five major regions of the country – north, south, east, west and central (see the map, overleaf, for more detail) – and a sense of the incredible diversity of flavours, ingredients, techniques and traditions that make Indian food so unique and vibrant.

By understanding the subtle (and not so subtle) nuances of the cuisine across India, you'll feel more confident to cook Indian food intuitively, adapt recipes to your taste, your mood or the time of year, and to cook more often.

My goal is to dispel the notion that Indian food is limited to just curries or a few familiar dishes on a typical restaurant menu.

I hope to inspire you to set out on a culinary adventure that promises to be one of the most exciting and rewarding experiences you could embark on, sparking an enthusiasm to further explore and cook more Indian food.

North

* Main states: Punjab, Haryana, Uttar Pradesh, Delhi and Kashmir.
* North Indian cooking is heavily influenced by the historical Mughal Empire, which introduced the use of aromatic and expensive spices and dried fruits.
* Fertile soils and pastures by riverbanks led to cattle farming and thus the wide use of dairy products. Beef isn't commonly eaten in this region, though.
* The tandoor clay oven hails from this region, so tandoori breads and kebabs are very common.
* Tangy chaats (see page 20), served by streetside hawkers, can be found across most cities and towns.
* Wheat is preferred to rice, making breads like parathas, naans and puris very popular.
* Iconic dishes include: chole, chaat, butter chicken, black dal, tandoori breads and kebabs.

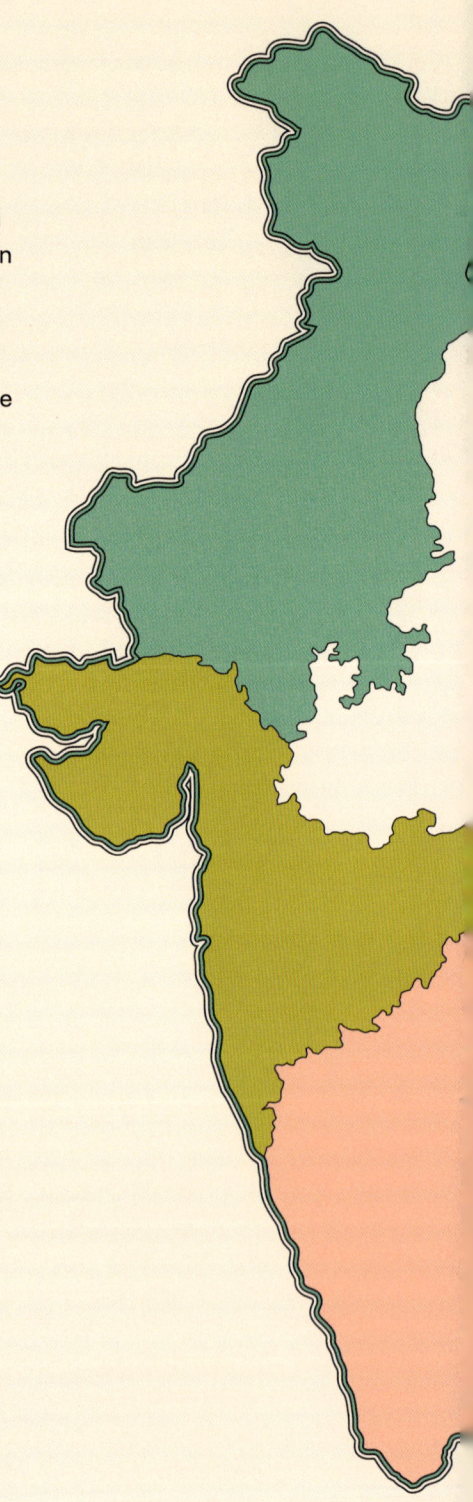

West

* Main states: Gujarat, Maharashtra, Rajasthan and Goa.
* There is a vast diversity in the dishes from the west:
  Gujarati food is predominantly vegetarian, and distinctly sweet.
  Maharastrian food favours fresh and dried seafood and lots of coconut and curry leaves.
  Rajasthani food features pickles, spices and meat, reflecting the desert terrain and the lack of fresh produce through most of the year.
  Goan food has distinct Portuguese influences.
* Iconic dishes: pickles, dhokla, pav bhaji, vindaloo and seafood curries.

East and North East

* Main states: West Bengal, Odisha, Assam, northeastern territories.
* Rice, mustard and fish play a big role in the cuisine of the east.
* Mustard oil and a slight sweetness even in savoury dishes is a hallmark of Bengali food.
* Food from the northeast is distinct and uses fermentation, and lighter spicing. Bamboo shoots, pork and influences from China play a big role here.
* Sweets made from curdled milk are popular.
   * Iconic dishes: mustard fish, baked yoghurt, aloo pitika, sandesh and momos.

Central

* Main states: Madhya Pradesh and Chhattisgarh.
* The cuisine of central Indian regions blends flavours and techniques from the neighbouring regions and heavily features lentils, wheat and millet.
* Iconic dishes: corn kees, poha.

South

* Main states: Tamil Nadu, Kerala, Karnataka, Andhra Pradesh and Telangana.
* India's vast southern coastline means that seafood, bananas and coconut are a big part of the diet in the south. Rice is preferred over wheat, and mustard seeds, tamarind, curry leaves and lentils play a big part in the cuisine.
* Dairy products are uncommon in the food of the south, and cattle are raised mainly for meat.
* Iconic dishes: dosas, biryanis, ishtews, banana leaf fish, and rice dishes, such as tamarind and lemon rice.

FLAVOUR HACKS

~~~~~~

Here are some tips and tricks to take your dishes to the next level, and save precious time in the kitchen while doing so. Much like the classic spice blends (see pages 266–68), many of these can be made ahead and are extremely versatile in their applications.

Ginger and Garlic

Most Indian recipes feature ginger and garlic. I always store a jar full of each, in paste form, in my fridge. Yet there are few ingredients I despise more than store-bought ginger and garlic pastes. They are full of unnecessary preservatives and ingredients, and taint dishes with a foul, synthetic flavour. Instead, I always make these pastes at home.

It only takes a couple of minutes to peel a handful of garlic cloves and a thumb-sized piece of ginger (use a spoon rather than a knife to peel ginger!), then blend them separately with a pinch of salt and a tablespoon of oil. They can be stored in airtight jars for up to a month. You can skip the oil, but this will reduce the shelf life to a few weeks.

If you're looking to stock up on these pastes, they freeze well and can be stored in bags or trays for months on end. Personally, I prefer to keep them refrigerated, as they are more convenient to use; and mine never last more than a few weeks anyway!

You can use garlic and ginger pastes when a recipe calls for grated versions of these, but you should adjust the quantities down slightly and remember that they will cook (and burn) a lot faster.

Onions

Onions play a crucial role in dishes. While frying them lightly can lend a delicate sweetness to a dish, cooking them to deep brown can both thicken a curry and give it a deep, caramelized flavour. Rich, meaty dishes often require this cumbersome step. You'll probably recognize the frequent instruction to 'cook your onions until golden brown' in Indian cookbooks, which puts many people off cooking curries.

Instead, I use a great hack that saves on time and delivers consistently effective results: a container of ready deep-fried onions.

Peel and finely slice some brown or red onions, wipe them dry and deep-fry small handfuls in a small wok filled with any neutral oil until deep golden brown and crisp. There's no need for any salt or flour, just plain onions. Remove them with a slotted spoon and spread them on kitchen paper to dry. Once cool, store them in an airtight jar or container, where they will keep for months.

Whenever a recipe calls for onions to be fried until golden brown, simply add about half the stated quantity of these pre-fried onions instead, along with a splash of water. Stir a few times and, in less than a minute, you'll be at the same stage it would have taken you the best part of 15–20 minutes to reach!

Red Chilli Paste

When I was growing up, my mum would always say that restaurants used food colourings to achieve their distinctive bright red tandoori chicken and curries. While this is sadly true a lot of the time, the secret behind the vibrant reds found in a lot of Indian food is often Kashmiri chilli. These chillies have a bright colour and are a lot milder on the heat scale.

Usually, good-quality Kashmiri chilli powder can do the trick, but for certain recipes, like Proper Butter Chicken (page 129), Pav Bhaji (page 68), Chilli Paneer (page 99) and a variety of Indo-Chinese dishes (such as Kung Pao Potatoes, page 57), using chilli paste takes the dish to new heights.

To make this at home, start by sourcing good-quality dried Kashmiri chillies (or Byadgi chillies). Remove the stems and seeds from 200g of dried chillies. Simmer them on a low heat in 1 litre of water for 25–30 minutes. Remove from the heat and leave to cool in the water. Once cooled completely, drain the water and blend the chillies in a food processor with a large pinch of salt and a tablespoon of oil.

This paste can be stored in a jar in the fridge for 2–3 weeks. If you plan to use the paste immediately, you can even skip the salt and oil, simply blending the chillies with a splash of water to achieve a bright-red paste.

Tarkas

Tarka, tadka, chonnk, vaghar, bhagar and popu are all regional terms for a universally vital step used in a whole host of Indian cooking. Fundamentally, it's the addition of a fresh layer of gently fried (tempered) aromatics and spices as the final step to a dish. At its simplest, it could involve frying a teaspoon of mustard or cumin seeds in a splash of ghee or oil and pouring it over a dish just before serving.

Adding fried garlic, dried or ground chillies, turmeric for a gorgeous golden hue, curry leaves, asafoetida, etc. are all very effective ways to amp up flavour and create a very relevant garnish.

The guide overleaf suggests some ideas to play with. Certain recipes may have a traditional tarka, but if you understand the rationale for it, you're welcome to use any number of the suggestions I've given to add flair to your dish.

Tarka Guide

Choose a fat and heat it over a medium heat	Veg oil (neutral and versatile) Mustard oil (for a pungent flavour, ideal for Bengali dishes) Ghee (for a buttery finish, ideal for dals and north Indian dishes) Coconut oil (a great vegan alternative for south Indian dishes)
Add hard spices first, cooking for about 15 seconds	Cloves Cinnamon Cardamom Bay leaves
Add seeds and cook until they begin to crackle	Mustard seeds Cumin seeds
Add ginger or garlic and cook on a low heat until golden	Minced or whole ginger or garlic
Add other spices and aromatics and cook on a medium heat for 10–15 seconds	Dried red chillies (whole, or broken and deseeded) Pandan leaves or lemongrass Fresh curry leaves Kasoori methi (dried fenugreek leaves)
Add ground spices and take off the heat to avoid burning them	Ground spices such as chilli, turmeric, coriander, cumin Asafoetida
Pour over the final dish just before serving	Save any leftovers in a jar for up to a week and reheat gently before using

Light
BITES

Potato Chaat

Serves 4

*****

**For the roasted potato
and chickpeas**

500g Maris Piper potatoes,
   peeled and cut into
   2.5cm cubes

3 tbsp neutral oil

½ tsp salt

1 x 400g tin of chickpeas, drained,
   rinsed and drained again

*****

For the yoghurt (optional)

200g Greek-style yoghurt,
   whisked

½ tsp black salt or sea salt

½ tsp sugar

½ tsp roasted and ground
   cumin seeds

*****

For the chaat

100g red onions, finely chopped

1 green chilli, finely chopped
   (optional)

2 tbsp Tangy Tamarind Chutney
   (store-bought, or see page 188)

2 tbsp Simple Green Chutney
   (see page 186)

1 tsp chaat masala (see page 266
   for homemade), plus more
   to sprinkle

½ tsp Kashmiri red chilli powder

½ tsp toasted cumin seeds,
   coarsely ground

2 tbsp chopped fresh coriander
   leaves

3–4 tbsp sev, to garnish

pomegranate seeds, to garnish
   (optional)

No book on Indian food would be complete without a recipe for chaat. *Chaat* literally translates as 'to lick' in Hindi. These dishes are typically eaten with your hands, and that irresistible urge to lick your fingers afterwards gave them the name – the original finger-lickin' food, long before the Colonel came along!

   This recipe is a perfect entry point, with crispy potatoes as the base, piled high with tangy, spicy and crunchy toppings. I roast or air-fry the potatoes for a lighter touch, but traditionally they're deep-fried. You can use store-bought tamarind chutney, but when it comes to green chutney, homemade is best – it takes a handful of ingredients and is ready in minutes. I like to freeze chutneys in small containers, so they're at hand whenever the chaat craving strikes.

1. Boil the potatoes for 6 minutes, then drain and let them rest for 8–10 minutes in the colander.

2. Toss the boiled potatoes with 2 tablespoons of oil and ½ teaspoon of salt. Air-fry in a single layer at 190°C for 20–25 minutes, or bake at 220°C fan for 30–35 minutes, turning halfway.

3. Meanwhile, coat the chickpeas in 1 tablespoon of oil. Add to the potatoes in the air fryer or oven halfway through the cooking time.

4. In a bowl, whisk together the yoghurt (if using) with the salt, sugar and cumin. Adjust the seasoning with more salt or sugar, if required.

5. As soon as the potatoes and chickpeas have roasted and are nice and golden, transfer them to a mixing bowl. Add the onions, green chilli, both types of chutney, the chaat masala, chilli powder, ground cumin and half the coriander leaves, and toss well.

6. Put the mixture into a serving bowl and drizzle or dollop the spiced yoghurt on top (if using). Sprinkle over the sev, pomegranate seeds and a large pinch of chaat masala, and finish with the remaining coriander leaves. Serve immediately to ensure that the potatoes remain crisp.

Chicken 65

Serves 4

*****

2½ tbsp cornflour

½ tsp ginger paste

½ tsp garlic paste

1 tsp Kashmiri red chilli powder

½ tsp ground turmeric

½ tsp ground black pepper

½ tsp salt, or to taste

500g boneless chicken thighs,
  cut into bite-size pieces

neutral oil, for deep-frying or
  air-frying

*****

For the tempering

2 tbsp neutral oil

½ tsp cumin seeds

10–12 curry leaves

2 green chillies, slit lengthways

1 tsp grated garlic

1 tsp grated ginger

2 tbsp red chilli paste
  (see page 15)

¼ tsp ground cumin

½ tsp ground black pepper

½ tsp MSG (optional, see
  page 256)

¼ tsp salt

juice of ½ lime or lemon

I haven't managed to pin down where this dish gets its name from. Various stories exist, but the most plausible one suggests that this chicken dish was the sixty-fifth item on the menu at a popular south Indian restaurant. A regular diner, unfamiliar with the local language, began to order it by its number rather than its name. Soon, others followed suit, and the dish became so popular that the number replaced its original name. Today, you can visit almost any south Indian restaurant and, regardless of the menu's length, Chicken 65 will most likely be on it.

1. In a large mixing bowl, combine the cornflour, ginger paste, garlic paste, chilli powder, turmeric, black pepper and ½ teaspoon of salt. Add the chicken pieces and mix well to coat evenly.

2. Heat the oil in a deep pan or wok over a medium-high heat. Once hot, add the marinated chicken pieces in batches, making sure not to overcrowd the pan. Fry until golden brown and crispy, about 5–6 minutes per batch. Remove with a slotted spoon and drain on kitchen paper. Alternatively, you can brush or spray the chicken pieces with oil and air-fry them at 190°C for 18–20 minutes, shaking the basket halfway through.

3. In a separate large pan, heat 2 tablespoons of oil over a medium heat. Add the cumin seeds and let them sizzle for a few seconds. Add the curry leaves and slit green chillies, and cook for a few seconds.

4. Add the grated garlic and ginger to the pan and cook for a minute until they begin to turn golden.

5. Stir in the Kashmiri chilli paste, cumin, black pepper, MSG (if using) and 50ml of water, along with ¼ teaspoon of salt. Cook for another minute, until the sauce thickens slightly.

6. Add the fried or air-fried chicken pieces to the pan and toss well to coat them evenly with the sauce. Cook for another 2–3 minutes, mixing well.

7. Squeeze the lime or lemon juice over the chicken and mix well. Serve immediately.

Bhajias

Serves 4–6

*****

250g gram flour

100g rice flour

¾ tsp ground turmeric

⅓ tsp Kashmiri red chilli powder

⅓ tsp baking powder

⅓ tsp cumin or carom seeds
  (optional)

1 tsp salt

1kg red onions

neutral oil, for deep-frying

Ask any Indian what snack comes to mind when the monsoons roll in, and the answer will be 'warm bhajias', enjoyed while watching the rain pour down. Popularly known as bhajis in the West, these are essentially fried vegetable fritters coated in a lightly spiced gram flour batter. They're perfect for teatime, especially when paired with a cup of masala chai or strong filter coffee.

Growing up, we made bhajias with just about anything: aubergines, potatoes, onions, fresh chillies, okra, bananas, and even mangoes. I know it sounds a bit wild, but if you're in the mood for something adventurous, try battering and frying some juicy ripe mango wedges – you'll be in for a treat.

This recipe is for the classic onion bhajias, but don't hesitate to switch things up and use whatever vegetable you fancy. Serve with some Simple Green Chutney (page 186) on the side.

1. In a large mixing bowl, combine the gram flour, rice flour, turmeric, chilli powder, baking powder, cumin seeds (or carom seeds) and ½ teaspoon of salt. Mix thoroughly and set aside.

2. Peel the onions, cut them in half lengthways and slice each half into 2–3mm thick slices.

3. Sprinkle the remaining salt over the sliced onions and mix thoroughly. Let the onions rest for about 10 minutes, allowing the salt to draw out excess moisture.

4. Gradually add half the dry mixture to the onions, mixing well. Add the rest of the dry mixture, massaging it into the onions until the mixture gets sticky and the onions are evenly coated. If the onions seem too dry and powdery, add a splash of water to the mix. Be sure to fry the onions immediately at this stage, to prevent them losing too much moisture.

5. Heat the oil to 170–180°C in a small wok, filling it no more than halfway up. Carefully lower a few battered onion slices into the hot oil, keeping the batter loose for a light, airy and crisp texture. Fry for 1–2 minutes, or until the bhajias are golden and crisp.

6. Serve them piping hot.

Bombay Sandwich

Serves 1

*****

2 slices of white bread

1 tbsp salted butter, softened

1 tbsp Simple Green Chutney
(page 186)

2–3 thin slices of ripe tomato

2–3 thin slices of potato, boiled
and peeled

2–3 thin slices of green pepper

2–3 thin slices of red onion

1 slice of cheese (Cheddar
or similar)

a large pinch of chaat masala
(see page 266 for homemade)

sev, to garnish (optional)

The Bombay sandwich, or cheese toastie, is a testament to the ingenious spirit of Indian street food culture, where street vendors take something foreign and transform it into a uniquely Indian creation, packed with spices and local flair, in such a way that you'd never imagine it existed in any other form previously.

Every street corner boasts a hawker grilling these sandwiches in camping toastie-makers over coal-fired stoves, each with their signature chutney or filling. One bite of these and you'll never settle for a plain cheese toastie again.

You can swap the boiled potatoes for a tablespoon of Potato Masala (page 162) or Mustard Mashed Potatoes (page 165). This is a great way to use up leftovers of those dishes and gives the sandwich an added layer of flavour. Serve with ketchup or Tangy Tamarind Chutney (page 188) for dipping.

1. Trim the crusts off the bread and butter each slice on both sides. You can use fancy bread, if you like, but the traditional version and the one I enjoy the most often uses simple, cheap, white sliced bread.

2. Build a sandwich in the following order, with a sprinkling of chaat masala every now and then to season the vegetables: bread – chutney – tomato – potato – green pepper – red onion – cheese – chutney – bread.

3. Toast in an electric or camping-style toastie-maker. If you're using a camping toastie-maker over an open flame, make sure you use a medium to low flame, and keep flipping the sandwich to ensure that the vegetables are fully cooked through and piping hot while the buttery toast turns a beautiful crisp golden brown.

4. Once toasted, spread some more chutney over both sides of the sandwich, scatter over some sev and serve.

Potato Tuk

Serves 2

*****

500g Maris Piper potatoes,
   peeled and cut into 1.5cm thick
   slices along the axis

neutral oil, for deep-frying

½ tsp ground turmeric

1 tsp Kashmiri red chilli powder

½ tsp ground cumin

½ tsp ground coriander

½ tsp ground black pepper

1 tsp chaat masala (see page 266
   for homemade)

salt

finely chopped fresh coriander,
   to garnish

juice of ½ lime, to garnish

This dish is a speciality of the Sindhi community from western India. If you've never tried tuk before, imagine the crunchiest triple-cooked chips, flattened and made crunchier still, then tossed in a mix of tangy spices. They are ridiculously moreish.

The potatoes are traditionally deep-fried, but you can cook them in an air fryer or an oven and achieve a very tasty result too. I recommend this for anyone who is nervous about deep-frying for health or safety reasons, or who, like me, ends up eating this dish too often. This can easily be doubled to serve four, but you might have to cook it in batches.

1. Soak the potato slices in salted water for 7–10 minutes, then drain and dry thoroughly with a clean kitchen cloth.

2. Fill a wide, round-bottomed wok or pan no more than a third with oil and heat to about 130°C (a round-bottomed pan saves on oil when frying). If you don't have a kitchen thermometer, heat the oil over a medium heat.

3. Carefully lower the potatoes into the oil with a slotted spoon to avoid splashes. Fry for about 10 minutes until a skewer penetrates them with no resistance and they are cooked through. They should only be a very light golden-yellow at this stage. If they begin to colour, your oil is too hot.

4. Cool the potatoes for 5 minutes in a sieve. You can make these up to 3–4 hours ahead and rest at room temperature until ready for the final fry.

5. Place the potatoes on a chopping board and carefully press them down one at a time with the base of a greased glass, flattening them to half their thickness, being careful not to break them apart. If the potato sticks, slice it off with a knife rather than trying to remove it by hand.

6. Raise the temperature of the oil to 190°C (or a medium-high heat). Deep-fry the potatoes until deep golden and crunchy, about 3–4 minutes. Depending on the size of your pan, you may need to fry the potatoes in batches to avoid the oil cooling down too much.

7. In a bowl, mix 2 tablespoons of hot oil from the pan with the spices. Remove the potatoes with a slotted spoon, draining them well against the side of the pan, and toss in the spiced oil.

8. Garnish with fresh coriander and a squeeze of lime. Serve immediately.

Alternative Air Fryer or Oven Method

1. Boil the potatoes in water for 6 minutes, then drain and dry thoroughly.

2. Coat the boiled potatoes generously in oil and either air fry at 160°C for 10 minutes or bake at 190°C fan for 13 minutes.

3. Press them down one at a time with the base of a greased glass, brush generously with more oil, and continue air frying or baking at maximum heat until crisp and golden (about 5–7 minutes).

4. To finish, mix all the spices together in a bowl and sprinkle over the potatoes, followed by the chopped coriander and a drizzle of lime juice.

Peanut Mudi Salad

Serves 4

*****

75g puffed rice

50g peanuts, roasted

100g tinned chickpeas or boiled
   dried chickpeas, drained

75g onions, finely chopped

100g cucumber, finely chopped

100g tomatoes, finely chopped

100g potatoes, boiled, peeled
   and cut into 1cm cubes

1 green chilli, finely chopped

1 tbsp chopped coconut pieces
   (optional)

3 tbsp finely chopped fresh
   coriander leaves

½ tsp salt, to taste

1½ tbsp mustard oil, or any
   neutral oil

juice of ½ lime or lemon

50g sev (optional)

*****

For the mudi masala

1 tsp fennel seeds

1 tsp cumin seeds

½ tsp coriander seeds

seeds from 2 green
   cardamom pods

Traditional Indian cookery doesn't feature many raw dishes, except for the ubiquitous Kachumber (page 176). I miss having salads with my meals, so I often turn to this popular streetside snack of puffed rice from Kolkata, loading it up with vegetables to create a salad of sorts. Feel free to substitute or add any vegetables you like to make it your own.

1. Start by making the mudi masala. In a dry wok over a medium heat, toast the fennel, cumin and coriander seeds for 2–3 minutes until fragrant. Remove from the heat and allow to cool. Once cooled, grind the toasted spices to a fine powder with the cardamom seeds, using a spice grinder or a pestle and mortar.

2. Wipe down the wok and toast the puffed rice over a medium-high heat for 2–3 minutes, until it becomes toasty and slightly charred in some spots.

3. In a large mixing bowl, combine the toasted puffed rice, roasted peanuts and drained chickpeas. Add the onions, cucumber, tomatoes, potatoes, green chilli, coconut pieces, fresh coriander and salt.

4. Drizzle in the mustard oil along with the lime or lemon juice, and add the freshly ground mudi masala. Mix everything thoroughly to ensure that all the ingredients are well combined and coated with the spices and oil.

5. Just before serving, sprinkle the sev (if using) on top for extra crunch. Serve immediately, as it will go soggy if left around for too long.

Bread Poha

Serves 2–3

*****

2 tbsp neutral oil

½ tsp black mustard seeds

½ tsp asafoetida (optional)

100g red onions, finely chopped

1 green chilli, finely chopped

8–10 curry leaves

¾ tsp ground turmeric

5–6 slices of white bread,
  crusts discarded, cut into
  1.5cm squares

50g frozen peas, cooked

½ tsp salt

1 tsp sugar

2 tsp finely chopped fresh
  coriander, to garnish

2–3 lime wedges, to serve

Poha is a very popular snack across western and central India and is traditionally made using flattened rice. However, this version, using white bread, is a favourite among students, especially those studying abroad with limited access to specialist ingredients and space to store them.

For a heartier version, you can add boiled, cubed potatoes and toasted peanuts, though I prefer to keep my bread poha plain. I love the hint of sweetness that a touch of sugar brings to the dish, but feel free to skip it if that's not to your taste.

1. Heat the oil in a pan over a medium heat. Add the mustard seeds and once they stop crackling, add the asafoetida, followed by the onions. Cook for 3–4 minutes, until the onions soften and turn translucent.

2. Add the green chilli, curry leaves and turmeric and cook for 30 seconds, stirring constantly.

3. Add the bread pieces and the cooked peas, along with the salt and sugar. If the bread is dry, add a splash of water, but be careful not to add too much as it will make the bread mushy. Mix everything well, making sure the bread is evenly coated with the spices. Continue cooking over a low heat for 4–5 minutes, until the bread starts to toast and becomes crispy in spots.

4. Serve immediately, garnished with fresh coriander and with a squeeze of lime juice.

Hara Kebabs

Makes 6–8

*****

500g baby spinach

200g fresh or frozen peas

1 tsp ghee

1½ tsp cumin seeds

2.5cm fresh ginger, grated

450g potatoes, boiled, peeled
   and roughly mashed

2 green chillies, finely chopped

½ tsp garam masala (optional)
   (see page 267 for homemade)

100g paneer, grated

2 tbsp finely chopped fresh
   coriander

2 tbsp finely chopped fresh mint
   leaves (optional)

juice of ½ lime

1 tsp salt

3 tbsp cashew nuts, toasted and
   roughly chopped (optional)

2 tbsp cornflour

3 tbsp oil, or as needed

1 tsp chaat masala (see page 266
   for homemade)

These vibrant green patties are a great addition to a kebab menu and are sure to keep both vegetarian and non-vegetarian guests happy. At home, we often serve them in a bun with some Tangy Tamarind Chutney (page 188) and Kachumber (page 176) as a quick veggie burger or slider. You can make the kebab mix up to a day ahead and then shape and fry them when ready to eat. Serve with a chutney of your choice, or even some ketchup.

1. Place the spinach in a pan of boiling water over a medium heat and cover. Let it cook for 1–2 minutes until it wilts completely, then immediately drain and transfer it to a bowl of iced water. This stops the cooking and helps preserve its vibrant colour. Once cooled, squeeze out excess water and blend the spinach to a smooth paste. If necessary, add a small amount of water to achieve a thick, smooth consistency, avoiding a soupy texture.

2. Cook the peas, boiling them for 5–6 minutes until tender if fresh (frozen peas will take less time to cook). Immediately transfer them to a bowl of cold water to cool. Once cooled, drain and roughly mash with a fork.

3. Heat the ghee in a non-stick pan over a medium heat. Add the cumin seeds and ginger, and fry for 2 minutes. Stir in the spinach paste and mashed peas and cook for about 5–6 minutes, until the mixture dries out.

4. Combine the cooked spinach and peas with the rest of the ingredients, except the cornflour, oil and chaat masala. Mix everything well until evenly and thoroughly combined. Taste and adjust the seasoning as required.

5. Shape the mixture into small patties, about 4cm in diameter. Lightly wet your hands to prevent sticking. Dust each patty with a little cornflour.

6. In a non-stick pan, heat the oil over a medium-high heat. Fry the patties for 4–5 minutes, turning them every 30–45 seconds to cook them evenly. Wipe the pan between batches, adding more oil as required.

7. Finish by sprinkling chaat masala over the patties, then serve.

Vada Pav

Serves 4

*****

For the potato filling

1 tbsp neutral oil

½ tsp mustard seeds

8–10 curry leaves

1 green chilli, finely chopped

½ tbsp ginger paste

½ tbsp garlic paste

1 tsp ground turmeric

300g Maris Piper potatoes,
 boiled, peeled and
 coarsely mashed

½ tsp salt

2 tbsp finely chopped fresh
 coriander leaves

*****

For the batter

100g gram flour

½ tsp ground turmeric

⅓ tsp Kashmiri red chilli powder

¼ tsp sea salt

*****

oil, to deep-fry

*****

For the garlic chutney

4–5 large garlic cloves, peeled

½ tsp Kashmiri red chilli powder

3 tbsp roasted skinless peanuts

2 tbsp desiccated coconut

½ tsp salt

*****

To serve

4 green chillies (optional)

pinch of salt (optional)

4 pavs or small brioche buns

2–3 tbsp Simple Green Chutney
 (page 186)

No dish captures the essence of Mumbai quite like the vada pav: entrepreneurial, quick, delicious and timeless. This bun stuffed with fried potato is a modest street food favourite among Mumbai's working class. Daily, millions savour it at streetside stalls, some of which have reached almost mythical status, drawing long lines of eager customers as the evening's first battered vadas plunge into sizzling oil.

A stellar vada pav hinges on a good vada – a batter-fried spiced potato fritter. But just as crucial are the fluffy pav buns and the vibrant chutneys that accompany it. My must-have inclusions are a tangy green chutney (page 186), a fiery garlic chutney (see below), plenty of crispy chura (see step 7, overleaf), and a fried whole green chilli.

1. Start by making the garlic chutney. Combine all the ingredients in a small electric grinder and pulse until you have a coarse red mixture. Transfer to a serving bowl and set aside.

2. To make the potato filling, heat the tablespoon of oil in a pan over a medium heat. Add the mustard seeds and, once they crackle, add the curry leaves and chopped green chilli. Stir for a few seconds until fragrant, then add the ginger and garlic pastes. Cook for 30 seconds, then sprinkle in the turmeric and stir well for a few seconds.

3. Add the coarsely mashed potatoes and mix everything well, seasoning with salt and stirring in the fresh coriander. Add a splash of water to bring everything together if required. Let it cool, then shape into 4 balls. Set aside.

4. For the batter, combine the gram flour, turmeric, chilli powder and salt in a mixing bowl. Slowly add 120ml water, whisking continuously until you get a thick, smooth batter that's the consistency of custard.

Method continues overleaf...

5. Heat enough oil for deep-frying in a wok or deep round-bottomed pan to about 160°C. You can test the oil with a drop of batter – it should sizzle gently and rise to the surface immediately, without burning. Dip each potato ball into the batter, making sure it's fully coated, then carefully drop it into the hot oil. Repeat with the other balls, trying not to overcrowd the pan. Depending on the size of your wok or pan, you may need to fry the vadas in two batches.

6. Fry each vada for 3–4 minutes, or until golden brown, flipping halfway through, then remove with a slotted spoon and drain on kitchen paper.

7. Once you've fried all the vadas, carefully drizzle in any remaining batter with a spoon, forming little balls and strands in the hot oil. Allow the batter to fry until crisp, about 3–4 minutes, then strain with a slotted spoon on to a plate lined with kitchen paper. We call these crispy bits chura, and they're great both as a snack on their own or added to the vada pav for extra crunch.

8. Finally, fry the whole green chillies (if using) in the hot oil for just 10–15 seconds, until blistered. Remove and season with a pinch of salt.

9. To build the vada pavs, slice each pav or bun in half. Spread some green chutney over both sides, then add a generous sprinkling of garlic chutney. Place a vada in the middle and top it with some chura and a fried chilli (if using), then close the bun tightly. Serve immediately, with more chura, chutneys and chillies on the side.

Instant Semolina Dosa

Makes 8–12 dosas, depending on the size of your pan

*****

75g fine semolina

75g rice flour

60g Greek-style yoghurt

½ tsp cumin seeds

1cm ginger, grated

40g onion, finely chopped

1 tbsp finely chopped fresh coriander

½ tsp salt

1 green chilli, finely chopped (optional)

3–4 tbsp neutral oil (or ghee or butter), to cook

Traditional folded dosas are a thing of beauty, but require planning and practice. These semolina dosas, on the other hand, can be made on a whim, in minutes, and require no more than a handful of ingredients and a non-stick pan. Known as rawa dosa, they are a legitimate version of dosas, not a shortcut for the more commonly known fermented rice and lentil dosas.

The cumin, ginger, onion and coriander add loads of flavour to the rawa dosa, but you could skip any or all of them, without compromising on the texture. *Pictured with Mum's Sambhar-style Dal (page 81).*

1. In a mixing bowl, combine all the ingredients except the oil and add 250ml of water. Whisk well until there are no lumps, then cover and let the batter rest for 10–15 minutes.

2. After resting, add 100–150ml of water to the batter until it reaches a very thin, milky consistency.

3. Heat a flat non-stick pan over a medium-high heat and add a few drops of oil. Once the oil shimmers, spread it evenly over the pan with a clean towel or kitchen paper.

4. Ladle some batter on to the pan. It should sizzle when added; if it doesn't, your pan isn't hot enough. The batter will spread across the pan and there may be some holes – this is normal.

5. Drizzle about ½ teaspoon of oil over the dosa. When the edges start to turn golden brown, which should take about 2–3 minutes, carefully peel off the dosa and serve immediately, folded in half. Typically, dosas are thin enough to cook on one side only, but if yours is slightly thicker and needs more time, you can flip it and cook it for an additional 30 seconds to a minute on the other side.

6. Wipe down the pan and repeat the process to make another dosa, stirring the batter very well each time. Any remaining batter can be stored in an airtight container in the fridge for up to a day. If you don't add the fresh coriander and onions, it can be stored for up to 3 days.

VEGETABLES
and
PULSES

Burnt Aubergine Bharta

Serves 2 as a main or 4 as a side

*****

2 large aubergines

2 tbsp mustard oil , plus extra
   for drizzling

1 tsp cumin seeds

160g onions, finely chopped

1½ tsp salt, to taste

1 tsp grated garlic

1 tsp grated ginger

1 tsp ground cumin

2 tsp Kashmiri red chilli powder

½ tsp ground turmeric

1 large ripe tomato, finely
   chopped (or ⅓ of a tin of
   chopped tomatoes)

½ tsp garam masala (see
   page 267 for homemade)

juice of ½ lime

1 tbsp finely chopped fresh
   coriander

1 green chilli, finely chopped,
   to garnish

The smell of aubergines roasting over an open fire always takes me back to memories of eating baingan bharta in Mumbai. Despite living in a block of flats, Baba, our cook, would set up a small charcoal grill by the window to grill the aubergines. Charring them over coal was crucial for the characteristic smoky flavour of the dish, and he wouldn't have it any other way. I don't recommend using live fire indoors, although thankfully we survived it. Ever since, I've adapted to my circumstances to grill aubergines over gas hobs, barbecues or directly under an oven grill.

Like many other Indian dishes, baingan bharta can vary dramatically from home to home. My version is based on a simple Punjabi recipe that uses mustard oil. If you don't have mustard oil or find its strong flavour too intense, you can easily swap it for a neutral oil.

1. Make a few small incisions in the aubergines with a sharp knife to allow the steam to escape when cooking. Rub a teaspoon or two of the mustard oil over them and roast over a flame or under the grill until they are completely charred and softened. You can use a barbecue, too. It takes about 15–20 minutes in an oven or on a hot barbecue, and a little less over a direct flame. Leave to cool, then peel the skin off and discard, along with any hard dry seeds inside. Chop the rest of the flesh finely and set aside.

2. Heat the rest of the mustard oil in a pan over a medium heat. Add the cumin seeds. Once they begin to crackle, add the onions along with ½ teaspoon of salt. Cook for 5–6 minutes, until softened, then add the ginger and garlic and cook for a further 3 minutes.

3. Add the cumin, chilli and turmeric and cook for 30 seconds, then add the tomato and cook for 5 minutes, adding a splash of water if the spices begin to stick to the pan. Once you have a thick spice paste, add the aubergine and simmer for 3–4 minutes, stirring and mashing everything together frequently. The final consistency should be similar to coarse mashed potato.

4. Add the garam masala, lime juice and fresh coriander along with 1 teaspoon of salt and cook for a final minute. Check the seasoning and serve garnished with chopped green chilli and a drizzle of mustard oil.

Okra and Potato Fry

**Serves 2 as a main
 or 4 as a side**

*****

300g okra

2½ tsp salt

2 tbsp neutral oil

500g Maris Piper potatoes,
   peeled and cut into 1cm cubes

½ tsp asafoetida

½ tsp ground turmeric

1 tsp Kashmiri red chilli powder

1 tsp ground cumin

2 tsp ground coriander

juice of ½ lime

If you're on the fence about okra, or find its slimy texture off-putting, this is a great dish to start with. It's easy to cook, with just a handful of ingredients, and stir-frying the okra ensures that it's fully cooked through and slime-free. Alternatively, swap the okra for aubergine cut into 1cm cubes for another delicious variation to this recipe. The aubergine will take a few minutes longer to cook than okra, so adjust the timing accordingly.

This dish is best enjoyed alongside some Simple Yellow Dal (see page 75), plain rice or Fulkas (see page 208).

1. Wash the okra and dry thoroughly. Cut the tops off and slice the okra widthways into 1cm slices. Place in a bowl and sprinkle over 1 teaspoon of the salt. Mix thoroughly and set aside while you prepare the rest.

2. Heat 1 tablespoon of oil in a large non-stick pan over a medium heat. Add the potatoes and ½ teaspoon of salt, stirring to coat the potatoes. Cover and cook, stirring occasionally, until the potatoes are cooked through but not brown, about 10–12 minutes. Remove the potatoes from the pan and set aside.

3. Using the same pan, add another tablespoon of oil. Add the asafoetida, followed by the okra, and cook uncovered over a medium heat for 5–6 minutes, until the okra have gone a shade darker and have lost their sliminess.

4. Return the cooked potatoes to the pan of okra. Add the turmeric, chilli powder, cumin, coriander and the remaining 1 teaspoon of salt. Stir well to combine all the spices with the vegetables.

5. Lower the heat and cook for 5–7 minutes, stirring occasionally, until the spices have fully coated the vegetables. Check the seasoning, squeeze over the lime juice, give it all a mix and serve hot.

Okra Yoghurt Curry

Serves 4 as a main

*****

300g okra

1 tsp salt

3 tbsp neutral oil

1 tsp cumin seeds

2 dried Kashmiri red chillies

150g onions, finely chopped

½ tsp ginger paste

½ tsp garlic paste

¼ tsp asafoetida

1 tsp Kashmiri red chilli powder

½ tsp ground turmeric

1 tsp ground cumin

2 tsp ground coriander

1 tsp kasoori methi (dried
   fenugreek leaves)

200g fresh ripe tomatoes,
   finely chopped (or 150g tinned
   chopped tomatoes)

250g Greek-style yoghurt

½ tsp garam masala (see
   page 267 for homemade)

juice of ½ lime (optional, if the
   yoghurt isn't already sour)

½ tsp sugar (optional, if the
   yoghurt is too sour)

This okra and yoghurt curry called dahi bhindi, from Rajasthan, has many variations. Some versions skip the onions and tomatoes, while others add pickling spices to the gravy for a unique riff. I love this version with plain rice or Puris (page 220).

Okra has often been overlooked in Western cooking because of its unfamiliarity. However, it's now widely available, and if cooked properly can be used in everything from stir-fries to curries, or even deep-fried in a light batter. To stop okra becoming slimy, I use three tricks: dry thoroughly before chopping, salt the chopped okra for 10–15 minutes before cooking and always cook uncovered.

1. Wash the okra and dry thoroughly with a clean towel. Cut the tops off and slice the okra into 5cm pieces. Place in a bowl and sprinkle over ½ teaspoon of the salt. Mix thoroughly and allow to sit for 10–15 minutes, then wipe dry with a clean tea towel or kitchen paper.

2. Heat 1 tablespoon of oil in a large non-stick pan over a medium heat. Add the okra and cook uncovered over a medium heat for 5–6 minutes until they have gone a shade darker and have lost their sliminess. Remove with a slotted spoon to a plate lined with kitchen paper.

3. Add another tablespoon of oil to the pan and heat over a medium heat. Add the cumin seeds and dried chillies and cook for a minute, then add the onions and a pinch of salt and cook until golden brown, about 6–8 minutes. Add the ginger and garlic and cook for a further minute.

4. Sprinkle in the asafoetida, chilli powder, turmeric, cumin, coriander and kasoori methi and cook for a minute, adding a splash of water, if required. Add the tomatoes and cook for 8–10 minutes until the oil begins to separate from the mixture.

5. Lower the heat to minimum. Whisk the yoghurt with about 150ml of water and add it to the pan, stirring continuously. Cook for 2 minutes, then add the fried okra, remaining salt and garam masala. Continue cooking for 4–5 minutes until the okra is soft but not breaking apart. Add a splash of water if you prefer the sauce thinner.

6. Check the seasoning and add lime juice or sugar to taste. Serve hot.

Bitter Gourd Fry

**Serves 2 as a main
or 4 as a side**
*****

400g bitter gourd
1 tsp salt
2½ tbsp neutral oil
½ tsp black mustard seeds
2 dried red chillies
10–12 whole cashews
2 tsp white sesame seeds
¼ tsp asafoetida
1 tsp Kashmiri red chilli powder
½ tsp ground turmeric
1 tsp ground cumin
1½ tsp ground coriander
1½ tsp sugar (optional)
juice of ½ lime (optional)

Bitter gourd is one of those fascinating vegetables that sparks strong reactions – people either shy away from it at the store, or have a clear love or dislike for it. Personally, I adore it and believe it's often misunderstood. When prepared properly, the bitterness can be balanced or mellowed, resulting in dishes that are truly unique.

The darker the bitter gourd, the more intense the bitterness tends to be. A useful tip is to salt the sliced bitter gourd for 15 minutes, then rinse it thoroughly to help reduce its bitterness. In many Gujarati households, you'll find recipes that incorporate generous amounts of sugar or jaggery to counterbalance the bitterness. I love this approach, and this Gujarati recipe is one we used to relish at my grandma's house regularly. Serve alongside a simple dal, Fulkas (page 208) or plain rice.

1. Cut off and discard the ends of the bitter gourd, and slice it into 2mm thin slices. Place in a bowl and sprinkle over ½ teaspoon of salt. Mix thoroughly and allow to sit for 10–15 minutes. After this time, wash thoroughly, squeezing the gourd with your hands to remove excess water. Wipe well with a clean tea towel or kitchen paper.

2. Heat 2 tablespoons of oil in a large non-stick pan over a medium heat and add the mustard seeds and dried red chillies. Once the mustard seeds begin to crackle, add the drained bitter gourd and the remaining salt and cook, stirring often, for 6–8 minutes, until the gourd is slightly crisp and fully cooked through.

3. Add the cashews and sesame seeds along with ½ tablespoon of oil and cook for a minute, until the cashews begin to change colour just slightly. Then add the asafoetida, chilli powder, turmeric, cumin and coriander, and cook for another minute. Keep stirring to ensure that the bitter gourd is evenly coated in all the spices.

4. If using the sugar and lime juice, add now and cook for a final minute, checking the seasoning to taste. Serve hot.

Alur Dom

Serves 2 as a main

*****

100g red onions, finely chopped

120g fresh ripe tomatoes,
  finely chopped (or 75g tinned
  chopped tomatoes)

1 tsp ginger paste

500g potatoes, peeled and cut
  into 2.5cm pieces

3 tbsp mustard oil,
  or any neutral oil

1 tsp cumin seeds

1 dried red chilli, stems and
  seeds removed

1 bay leaf

½ tsp ground turmeric

2 green chillies, slit lengthways

½ tsp Kashmiri red chilli powder

1 tsp ground coriander

½ tsp ground cumin

½ tsp salt, to taste

1 tsp sugar

People in Kolkata are crazy for potatoes, and this dish is a firm favourite. It's so simple, and a wonderful Sunday lunch alongside freshly fried Luchis (page 219) and Spicy Fried Aubergine (page 166). You can make this dish with new potatoes, baby potatoes or large potatoes that have been cut into cubes.

1. Blend together the onions, tomatoes and ginger to make a fine paste.

2. Wash the potatoes in running water to get rid of the excess starch and drain well.

3. Heat 2 tablespoons of mustard oil in a pan set over a medium heat and add the cumin seeds, dried red chilli and bay leaf. After a minute, add the potatoes and fry for 6–8 minutes, until they start to turn light golden. Add the turmeric and fry for another minute, then transfer the potatoes to a plate with a slotted spoon.

4. In the same pan, add the remaining 1 tablespoon of mustard oil and heat over a medium heat, then add the tomato paste and fry for 6–8 minutes until the oil begins to separate to the surface. Add the potatoes, green chillies and the rest of the ground spices and fry for 2–3 minutes, then add 500ml of water, to cover the potatoes. Put a lid on the pan and cook on a low heat for 20–30 minutes, or until the potatoes have cooked through and a knife or skewer pierces them with ease.

5. Add the salt and sugar, mix well and cook for a final 2 minutes. Check the seasoning and serve.

Kung Pao Potatoes

Serves 4 as a starter

*****

500g frozen potato wedges or
   chips (see right)

1 tbsp neutral oil

1 tsp grated ginger

2 tsp grated garlic

3–4 spring onions, finely
   chopped and separated into
   white and green

2 green chillies, slit in
   half lengthways

2 tbsp tomato ketchup

2 tbsp red chilli paste
   (see page 15) or 1 tsp Kashmiri
   red chilli powder

2 tsp dark soy sauce

1 tsp white vinegar
   (rice or white wine)

½ tsp ground white or
   black pepper

a pinch of MSG (optional, see
   page 256)

1 tbsp cornflour, mixed with
   200ml water

1 tsp salt, to taste

Indo-Chinese food is hugely popular in Mumbai. Historically, as the city grew and waves of Chinese immigrants brought their own cooking styles with them, so meals were adapted to suit local tastes. This dish is a standard order for me at any Indo-Chinese restaurant or streetside stall in Mumbai. It's got everything to love, and more: crispy potatoes, tossed in a garlicky, sweet and spicy sauce, topped with piles of spring onions. A favourite among meat eaters and vegans alike, this dish is a great example of Chinese flavours masterfully adapted for the Indian palate.

I use store-bought freezer chips or wedges for this when I'm in a hurry, but you can easily make them at home: dust sliced potatoes with a pinch of salt and cornflour, then deep-fry over a medium heat until golden, about 10–12 minutes. Drain well, then follow the recipe from step 2 below.

1. Cook the potato wedges according to the packet instructions and set them aside while you prepare the sauce.

2. Heat the oil in a wok over a medium heat and stir-fry the ginger and garlic for a minute or two until golden and aromatic, being careful not to let them burn. Add the spring onion whites, green chillies, tomato ketchup, chilli paste or powder, soy sauce, vinegar, pepper and MSG. Cook for about 2 minutes, then add the cornflour mixture. Continue cooking for 4–5 minutes, stirring constantly, until the sauce is thick and glossy.

3. Add the potatoes and salt and cook for 2 minutes until the potatoes are piping hot.

4. Garnish with the spring onion greens and serve immediately.

Aloo
Matar

Serves 2 as a main

*****

4 medium potatoes, peeled and
   cut into 4cm cubes

1 tbsp vegetable oil or ghee

1 tsp cumin seeds

2 bay leaves

80g red onions, finely chopped

up to 2 tsp salt, to taste

1 tsp each grated ginger
   and garlic

1 tsp ground turmeric

1 tsp Kashmiri red chilli powder

½ tsp ground cumin

¾ tsp ground coriander

150g ripe fresh tomatoes, finely
   chopped (or 120g tinned
   chopped tomatoes)

150g frozen peas

1 tbsp chopped fresh coriander,
   plus more to garnish

juice of ½ lime

This simple, quick and incredibly delicious potato and pea curry is a staple in homes across India, particularly in the north. I love eating it with plain rice, Puris (page 220) or Fulkas (page 208) drizzled with ghee. It epitomizes Indian home cooking and showcases the contrast between simple, tasty food cooked at home versus the richer, restaurant-style dishes often associated with Indian cuisine. While both have their place, if you're unfamiliar with the former, this is a great recipe to start with.

   People usually boil potatoes before adding them to curries or stir-fries, but I've found that boiling them in the gravy gives them a much deeper flavour. I use Maris Pipers, but any good all-purpose potato will work well.

1. Wash the potatoes in running water to get rid of the excess starch and drain well. Set aside.

2. Heat the oil in a pan set over a medium heat and add the cumin seeds. Once they crackle, add the bay leaves and the onions, with ½ teaspoon of salt to ensure they cook evenly.

3. Once the onions have softened, add the ginger and garlic and fry everything for a couple of minutes.

4. Add the spices and fry for 30 seconds. Then add the tomatoes and cook, stirring occasionally, until they become thick and some of the oil rises to the surface, about 8–10 minutes.

5. Add the potatoes, along with enough water just to cover them. Put a lid on the pan and cook on a low heat for 15–20 minutes, or until the potatoes have cooked through and a knife or skewer pierces them with ease.

6. Add the peas and cook for another 3–4 minutes.

7. Stir in the chopped coriander and lime juice and check the seasoning, adding more salt as needed. Serve, garnished with more fresh coriander.

Corn Kees

**Serves 4 as a snack
 or side**

*****

300g sweetcorn, boiled, tinned
 (drained), or fully defrosted
 if frozen

1½ tbsp neutral oil, ghee or
 butter

½ tsp black mustard seeds

½ tsp cumin seeds

¼ tsp asafoetida (optional)

1 green chilli, finely chopped

2.5cm ginger, grated

8–10 curry leaves (optional)

½ tsp ground turmeric

100ml whole milk, vegan
 alternative or water

½ tsp salt

1 tsp sugar (optional)

1 tbsp finely chopped fresh
 coriander leaves, to garnish

1 tbsp grated coconut,
 to garnish

Bhutte ka kees is a popular corn dish from Indore, in the central Indian state of Madhya Pradesh, which is usually enjoyed during the monsoon season when corn is abundant. This dish, an Indian polenta of sorts, is traditionally made with the local corn, which is not as sweet as the sweetcorn found in the West, so you can skip adding sugar if using the latter. *Kees* means 'grated', which is how this dish is traditionally prepared. It's usually enjoyed as a snack on the streets, but can also be eaten for breakfast.

1. Start by grating the corn, using a grinder or food processor, until coarsely ground. If you're using frozen corn, thaw it completely first. Make sure you grind the corn carefully, as you don't want to make a paste. The corn should retain some texture.

2. Heat the oil, ghee or butter in a non-stick pan over a medium heat. Add the mustard seeds and cumin seeds. When the mustard seeds start to crackle, add the asafoetida, green chilli and ginger, and the curry leaves (if using), and cook for 2 minutes.

3. Add the turmeric and cook for 15–20 seconds, then add the corn and cook for 4–5 minutes, stirring occasionally.

4. Pour in the milk and bring to a simmer. Reduce the heat to low and cook, stirring frequently for 6–8 minutes, until most of the milk has been absorbed. Add the salt and sugar (if using), and a little more milk or water if you prefer the consistency runnier.

5. Check that you are happy with the seasoning, cook for a final minute and serve garnished with finely chopped coriander and grated coconut.

Green Bean Poriyal

Serves 2 as a side

*****

1½ tbsp coconut oil, or any neutral oil

½ tsp black mustard seeds

½ tsp husked raw black lentils

¼ tsp asafoetida (optional)

2 dried red chillies, stems and seeds removed

8–10 curry leaves

400g green beans, cut into 1cm pieces

1 tsp salt, to taste

75g grated coconut

1 lime, cut into wedges, to serve

A poriyal is a simple stir-fried dish popular in Tamil Nadu, a state in South India. This everyday dish typically features seasonal vegetables, such as carrots, cabbage, beans, beetroot and okra, lightly stir-fried with freshly grated coconut and a handful of spices. You can substitute the green beans in this recipe with any of these vegetables. The cooking time will vary depending on the vegetable used and how it is cut.

1. Heat the coconut oil in a pan over a medium heat. Add the mustard seeds and raw lentils. Once the lentils turn light brown and smell nutty, add the asafoetida, chillies and curry leaves and stir for a few seconds until fragrant.

2. Add the green beans, salt and 50g of the grated coconut to the pan. Mix everything thoroughly to combine, then add about 3 tablespoons of water, cover with a lid and allow the beans to steam for about 4 minutes. Uncover and continue cooking until the water evaporates fully.

3. Check the seasoning, and serve the beans immediately, garnished with the remaining coconut and with a wedge of lime on the side.

Tandoori-style Whole Roast Cauliflower

Serves 4 as a main

*****

1 large cauliflower, leaves
removed

2 tsp ground turmeric

2 tsp salt

Simple Green Chutney (see
page 186), to serve

*****

For the tandoori marinade

3 tbsp melted butter

100g Greek-style yoghurt

100g cream cheese

½ tsp ginger paste

½ tsp garlic paste

2 tsp Kashmiri red chilli powder

½ tsp garam masala (see
page 267 for homemade)

1 tbsp lime juice

1 tsp kasoori methi (dried
fenugreek leaves)

1 tsp salt

1 tsp chaat masala (see page 266
for homemade)

I love the theatre of presenting a whole roasted cauliflower as the centrepiece at a dinner party. Cauliflower tends to have a bad reputation because it's so often overcooked. But roasting is a fantastic way to prepare it – it keeps the flavour intact and avoids that unpleasant, sulphuric smell you get from over-boiling it.

If you're still not convinced, the marinade I've used here isn't just for cauliflower – it works just as well with broccoli, potatoes, paneer, chicken, or even lamb chops. It's that classic red marinade that's synonymous with tandoori dishes, though unless you're cooking in an actual tandoor, it's not quite accurate to call it tandoori.

1. Preheat your oven to 190°C fan. In a large bowl, mix all the ingredients for the tandoori marinade, saving 2 tablespoons of butter to brush the cauliflower.

2. Fill a large saucepan with water and bring it to the boil. Add 2 teaspoons of turmeric and 2 teaspoons of salt, then carefully immerse the cauliflower in the water and allow it to simmer for 3–4 minutes. Carefully drain away the water and place the cauliflower in a large bowl filled with chilled water, or under running water, to stop it cooking further. Once cool, drain the cauliflower well and place it in a bowl.

3. Drizzle 1 tablespoon of melted butter over the cauliflower, then coat it thoroughly with the marinade, making sure the marinade gets everywhere, especially into the crevices. Reserve the leftover marinade for later.

4. Place the marinated cauliflower on a tray lined with baking parchment. Roast for 15 minutes, then remove and brush a second layer of marinade over the cauliflower. Increase the oven temperature to 200°C fan and return the cauliflower to the oven for a further 10–15 minutes, or until it is cooked through and nicely charred on the outside. Check for doneness by inserting a knife into the core – it should go through easily.

5. Remove the cauliflower from the oven, drizzle over the reserved melted butter, sprinkle over the chaat masala, and serve with the green chutney on the side or drizzled all over.

Tomato and Tamarind Rasam

Serves 2 as a starter
or soup

*****

60g split red lentils (masoor dal)

1 tsp cumin seeds

½ tsp black peppercorns

2 dried red chillies, stems and
seeds removed (I use Byadgi
or Guntur chillies)

3 garlic cloves

8–10 curry leaves

a handful of fresh coriander,
stems and leaves

500g ripe fresh tomatoes, finely
chopped (or 350g tinned
chopped tomatoes)

3–4 tbsp freshly made tamarind
paste (see page 259)
or juice of 1½ limes

2 tsp salt, to taste

fresh coriander leaves,
to garnish

*****

For the tarka

1½ tbsp vegetable oil

½ tsp black mustard seeds

½ tsp cumin seeds

¼ tsp fenugreek seeds
(optional)

¼ tsp asafoetida

½ tsp Kashmiri red chilli powder

8–10 curry leaves

This simple south Indian soup is perfect any time of the day or year, with boiled rice, as part of a larger meal, or simply sipped from a cup. It is warming, packed with flavour, healthy and quick to make. There are hundreds of variations of this dish across south India, but this is the version I grew up eating and it's my go-to.

Using very ripe (even overripe) soft tomatoes is crucial for this recipe. If you don't have ripe tomatoes, use tinned and add some extra tamarind, as tinned tomatoes tend to be sweeter than fresh ones. The extra sourness from the tamarind will balance out the sweetness. If you can't find tamarind, add the juice of 1½ limes just before serving instead.

1. Wash the lentils until the water runs almost clear. Place them in a deep pan with 1 litre of water and boil until soft and mushy, about 15–20 minutes. If you have a pressure cooker, this step can be done even faster.

2. Toast the cumin seeds, peppercorns and dried chillies in a dry pan over a medium heat for about a minute. Once cooled, grind them with the garlic and curry leaves to make the masala. You can use a pestle and mortar or toss it all into an electric spice grinder. Try to keep the mix coarse, don't grind it all to a paste. I use a pestle and mortar for the best texture.

3. Roughly chop the coriander stems and put them into a mixing bowl with the ground masala. Chop the tomatoes roughly and add them to the bowl. Using your hands, crush everything to a coarse pulp. You can use a blender for this, if you prefer, but many south Indian cooks swear by the fact that using your hands to crush the tomatoes adds more flavour to the dish!

4. When the lentils have cooked, add the crushed tomato mix to the boiled lentils along with the tamarind, 1 litre of water and 2 teaspoons of salt. Bring everything to a gentle simmer and cook for 15–20 minutes on a medium-low heat to allow the flavours to infuse. Check that you're happy with the balance of flavours, adding more tamarind or salt if you like. You can strain the rasam or serve it as is. I prefer all the bits left in.

5. When ready to serve, heat the oil in a small pan and add the ingredients for the tarka. Cook for 30 seconds, then pour it over the rasam. Stir well and serve in bowls or cups, garnished with fresh coriander.

Pav
Bhaji

Serves 2 as a main

*****

4 large dried Kashmiri red
    chillies, seeds removed
    (or 2 tsp Kashmiri red
    chilli powder)

2 tbsp butter, plus more
    to serve

1 tsp cumin seeds

1 small (100g) red onion, finely
    chopped, plus more to serve

1½ tsp salt

½ tbsp ginger paste

½ tbsp garlic paste

3 ripe medium tomatoes, finely
    chopped (or 200g tinned
    chopped tomatoes)

1½ tbsp pav bhaji masala
    (spice blend available at Asian
    grocery stores)

1 medium (150g) potato, boiled
    and roughly chopped

2 tbsp frozen peas, cooked

1 tbsp chopped fresh coriander
    leaves, to garnish

4 small pav or brioche buns,
    to serve

3–4 lime wedges, to serve

If I had to choose one dish that truly represents my hometown of Mumbai, it would be this one. A classic at street food stalls and restaurants all over the city, this wonderful spiced vegetable mash is a true leveller, bringing together people from all walks of life, different classes, castes, religions and backgrounds – side by side in sheer enjoyment.

Like any good mash, butter plays a vital role here – the more you use the tastier the result. Equally essential is the pav. Pav is arguably the most affordable bread in Mumbai. It's similar to a brioche bun but much lighter and fluffier. Since it's hard to find authentic pav outside Mumbai, I often use soft brioche buns as a quick substitute.

1. Begin by soaking the dried chillies in hot water for 30 minutes. Once softened, drain and grind them into a smooth paste, using some of the soaking water if needed. If dried Kashmiri chillies aren't available, you can substitute Kashmiri red chilli powder. Avoid using other dried chillies, as they may be much spicier.

2. In a large pan, heat the butter over a medium heat. Add the cumin seeds, and when they start to crackle, stir in the onion with a pinch of salt. Cook for 6–8 minutes, until the onion softens and turns light brown, then add the ginger and garlic pastes and cook for another minute.

3. Add the tomatoes and cook for 5–7 minutes, until you notice small bubbles of fat on the surface. Stir in the pav bhaji masala and the chilli paste (or powder), followed by the potato and peas. Pour in 150–200ml of water and continue cooking, mashing the vegetables with a fork or masher until they break down and combine into a cohesive mash.

4. Transfer the bhaji to a serving bowl and garnish with a dollop of butter and the chopped coriander leaves.

5. Slice the pav or brioche buns in half, then fry them in a hot pan for 10–15 seconds with melted butter until they begin to turn golden.

6. Serve the pav alongside the bhaji, with finely chopped onions and lime wedges for sprinkling and drizzling on top.

Chole

Serves 4–6 as a main

*****

200g dried chickpeas
  (or 2 x 400g tins of chickpeas,
  drained and rinsed)

1–2 tea bags

½ tsp bicarbonate of soda,
  if using dried chickpeas,
  or 1 pinch, if using tinned

2 tbsp ghee or neutral oil

2 bay leaves

2.5cm cinnamon stick

3 green cardamom pods

150g onions, thinly sliced

1½ tsp salt, to taste

1 tsp garlic paste

2 tsp ginger paste

2 green chillies, slit lengthways

200g fresh ripe tomatoes,
  finely chopped (or 80g tinned
  chopped tomatoes)

½ tsp ground turmeric

1 tsp ground cumin

1 tsp ground coriander

1 tsp garam masala (see
  page 267 for homemade)

1 tsp Kashmiri red chilli powder

1 tsp aamchur (see page 255), or
  the juice of ½ lime

2 tbsp chopped fresh coriander,
  to garnish

5cm ginger, cut into matchsticks,
  to garnish

Chole is a Punjabi chickpea curry that's arguably one of the most beloved street food dishes, eaten with fluffy Bhaturas (page 223), Puris (page 220) or Fulkas (page 208). I recommend using good-quality large dried chickpeas, as soaking and boiling them with spices ensures they absorb all the flavours and develop a wonderful light texture. If you can't find good dried chickpeas or are short of time, be sure to drain and rinse tinned chickpeas thoroughly. Then give them a quick boil, as they tend to be quite firm straight out of the tin. For this dish, it's best to have soft chickpeas, as some are mashed into the gravy to add body. The tea bags give the chickpeas their characteristic dark colour but don't significantly affect the flavour, so leave them out if you prefer.

1. If using dried chickpeas, soak them in water overnight. Drain and rinse them the following day, then put them into a large pot with the tea bags and bicarbonate of soda. Cover the chickpeas with 1.5 litres of fresh water and cook over a medium heat until soft, about 1–1½ hours. (This can be done in about half the time in a pressure cooker.) Discard the tea bags and allow the chickpeas to cool.

2. If using tinned chickpeas, drain and rinse them, then put them into a large pot with 600ml of fresh water, 1 tea bag and a pinch of bicarbonate of soda. Cook over a medium heat for 15–20 minutes, or until soft enough to split when you press them. Discard the tea bag and save the water.

3. Heat the oil in a large pan over a medium heat and add the bay leaves, cinnamon and cardamom. Let them sizzle for a few seconds until fragrant.

4. Add the onions along with a pinch of salt and cook for 10–12 minutes, until golden brown. To save time here, you can use 2 tablespoons of fried brown onions along with a splash of water (see page 12 for more). Add the garlic paste, ginger paste and green chillies, and cook for another 2–3 minutes.

5. Add the finely chopped tomatoes and cook until they break down and the oil starts to separate from the mixture, about 6–8 minutes.

6. Add the turmeric, cumin, ground coriander, garam masala, chilli powder and the remaining salt. Stir well to combine and cook for 2–3 minutes, until the spices are well incorporated.

7. Add the drained chickpeas to the pan and stir to coat them in the spice mixture. Add about 300ml of the chickpea water and bring to the boil, then lower the heat and let the chickpeas simmer for 10–12 minutes until most of the water has been absorbed. Keep stirring and mashing some of the chickpeas – this helps thicken the sauce wonderfully. Once you are happy with the consistency and texture of the dish, add the aamchur and adjust the seasoning if required, then cook for a final 2 minutes.

8. Garnish with the fresh coriander and ginger, and serve hot.

Black Dal

**Serves 4 as a main or
6 as a side**

*****

225g dried black lentils

3 tbsp ghee or butter

5 green cardamom pods

5cm cinnamon stick

2 tsp ginger paste

2 tsp garlic paste

2 tsp Kashmiri red chilli powder

2½ tsp ground coriander

1½ tsp ground cumin

500g tomatoes, finely chopped
(or 400g tinned chopped
tomatoes)

150g cooked kidney beans (or
400g tinned kidney beans,
drained)

2 tsp kasoori methi (dried
fenugreek leaves)

100g double cream, plus more
to garnish

2–3 green chillies, slit

2½ tsp salt, to taste

Dal is a word used to describe both the raw lentil and dishes cooked with lentils. Raw black lentils are known as urid dal, and the omnipresent dish cooked with them, found at every north Indian restaurant, is known as kali dal or dal makhani. There are as many versions of cooked dals as there are permutations and combinations of dried lentils. That said, a good black dal is possibly my favourite. It's a labour of love, and is best slow-cooked over several hours. I know of restaurants where the dish is famously cooked over days. At home, I cook a large pot of it on weekends when I have other things to do in the kitchen, allowing it to cook in the background for hours on end. The final product is then carefully boxed away and frozen, to be served as a side at special dinners or as a main dish alongside some rice, parathas or naans on weeknights when we are after something comforting.

1. Wash the lentils thoroughly and soak them in 3 litres of water overnight. They will expand, so ensure you use a large bowl. Drain and rinse the lentils the next day, then transfer them to a large pot with 4 litres of water. Cook, covered, over a medium heat until tender, about 1–1½ hours. You can use a pressure cooker to reduce the cooking time to 30–40 minutes. Make sure the lentils have softened completely and break apart when gently squeezed between your fingers. If they haven't cooked through at this stage, they won't break down further once the other ingredients are added.

2. Heat the ghee or butter in a large pan over a medium heat. Add the cardamom and cinnamon and cook for a minute until fragrant, then add the ginger and garlic and cook for a further minute. Stir in the chilli powder, coriander and cumin and cook for another minute.

3. Add the tomatoes to the pan and cook for 8–10 minutes until the oil begins to separate from the mixture.

4. Add the lentils along with 350ml of their cooking liquid or water and stir well. Add the kidney beans and the kasoori methi and cook for 5 minutes. Reduce the heat, add the cream, then simmer for 15–20 minutes, stirring constantly and mashing some of the lentils and beans with the back of the spoon to thicken the dish. Take it off the heat when the lentils have softened completely and the dish has reached your desired consistency.

5. Add the green chillies and salt, adjusting to taste. Garnish with a drizzle of cream and serve hot.

Simple Yellow Dal

**Serves 4 as a main or
6 as a side**

*****

350g split yellow lentils
(mung dal)

1½ tsp ground turmeric

3 tbsp neutral oil

1½ tsp cumin seeds

1 tsp asafoetida

10–12 curry leaves

4cm ginger, grated

3 garlic cloves, finely grated

150g fresh tomatoes,
finely chopped

2–3 green chillies,
split lengthways

2 tsp salt, or to taste

2 tbsp finely chopped fresh
coriander leaves

This mung dal was served at lunch almost every day at my grandma's home. We would eat it alongside some lightly spiced stir-fried sprouts, okra, fulkas and plain rice liberally topped with homemade ghee. It's one of the quickest and easiest dals you can make and requires very little planning ahead, as yellow lentils don't need to be soaked before cooking.

To turn this into a complete meal, simply add some washed and roughly chopped spinach leaves a couple of minutes before taking it off the heat, and enjoy with some plain rice or Fulkas (page 208).

1. Wash the lentils thoroughly in several changes of water until the water runs somewhat clear, then drain. Put the lentils into a large pot with the turmeric and 2 litres of water. Bring to the boil, then reduce the heat to medium-low and simmer, uncovered, for 20–25 minutes until the lentils are tender and fully cooked.

2. Heat the oil in a large pan over a medium heat, then add the cumin seeds and cook for a minute until they begin to crackle. Add the asafoetida, curry leaves, ginger and garlic, and cook for a further minute.

3. Add the cooked lentils to the pan, along with any cooking liquid, and mix well. Bring the mixture to a gentle boil, then reduce the heat and add the tomatoes, green chillies and salt. Simmer for 10–15 minutes, adding more water if required to reach your desired consistency. Check the seasoning and adjust if necessary.

4. Garnish with the coriander and serve.

Punjabi Rajma

Serves 2 as a main

*****

125g dried kidney beans, or
   250g tinned kidney beans
   (drained weight)

¼ tsp baking powder

60g onions, finely sliced

250g tomatoes, finely chopped
   (or 200g tinned chopped
   tomatoes)

1 tsp garlic paste

1 tsp ginger paste

2 tbsp neutral oil or ghee

1 star anise

1 bay leaf

2 green cardamom pods

2.5cm cinnamon stick

¾ tsp Kashmiri red chilli powder

1 tsp ground coriander

½ tsp garam masala (see
   page 267 for homemade)

1 green chilli, slit lengthways

1 tsp salt, to taste

2 tbsp finely chopped fresh
   coriander, to garnish

Kidney beans, often known as rajma, are the star of this traditional Punjabi-style stew. A favourite in our household, this dish easily ranks in our top three weeknight meals. I frequently cook a large batch and freeze portions, ensuring we always have some to hand when the craving strikes.

Soaking dried kidney beans and cooking them from scratch always delivers the best results, but if you're in a hurry you can use tinned beans. Drain and rinse them before using and adjust the seasoning of the dish accordingly, as tinned beans can be fairly salty. Serve with plain rice.

1. *If using dried kidney beans:* wash them thoroughly and soak them in 1 litre of water overnight – they will expand, so make sure you use a large bowl. The next day, drain and rinse the beans, then transfer them to a large pot with the baking powder and 2 litres of water and cook covered over a medium heat until tender, about 1–1½ hours. You can use a pressure cooker to reduce the cooking time to about 30–40 minutes. Make sure the beans have softened completely and break apart when gently squeezed between your fingers. If they haven't cooked through at this stage, they won't break down further once the remaining ingredients are added. Once fully cooked, drain the kidney beans and reserve the cooking liquid separately.

If using tinned kidney beans: just drain and rinse the beans.

2. Blend the onions, tomatoes, garlic and ginger pastes to a smooth paste.

3. Heat the oil or ghee in a large pan over a medium heat. Add the star anise, bay leaf, green cardamom pods and cinnamon and cook for a minute until fragrant, then add the chilli powder and ground coriander and cook for another minute.

4. Add the onion/tomato paste to the pan and cook for 8–10 minutes until the oil begins to separate from the mixture. Add the beans and stir to coat them in the masala. Add enough of the reserved cooking liquid or water to cover the beans and bring to the boil, then reduce the heat and let the beans simmer for 10–15 minutes until they soften completely and the gravy reaches your desired consistency. I like my rajma fairly thick, but you can adjust the consistency to your preference.

5. Add the garam masala, green chilli and salt, adjusting to taste, then garnish with freshly chopped coriander and serve hot.

Dhaba Dal Fry

**Serves 4 as a main or
6 as a side**

*****

350g split yellow gram
(chana dal)

2 tsp ground turmeric

3 tbsp neutral oil or ghee

2 tsp cumin seeds

3–4 dried red chillies, stems and
seeds removed

1 tsp asafoetida

200g onions, finely chopped

1½ tbsp ginger paste

1½ tbsp garlic paste

1 tsp Kashmiri red chilli powder

2 tsp ground coriander

350g fresh tomatoes, finely
chopped (or 360g tinned
chopped tomatoes)

1 tsp garam masala (see
page 267 for homemade)

2 tsp salt, or to taste

2–3 tbsp chopped fresh
coriander leaves, to garnish

wedges of lime or lemon,
to serve

Dhabas are roadside eateries found alongside roads and highways across northern India. This dal is as popular among the truckers that frequent these dhabas as black dal is at Indian restaurants in the West. I love the texture and flavour of the split yellow gram (chana dal), a cousin of the chickpea, that's used in this dish. This hearty dal pairs beautifully with Parathas (page 216), Naans (page 224), Fulkas (page 208) or plain rice.

1. Wash the gram thoroughly in several changes of water until the water runs somewhat clear. Soak in fresh water for 3–4 hours, or ideally overnight.

2. Put the soaked, drained gram into a large pot and add the turmeric and 2.5 litres of water. Bring to the boil, then reduce the heat to medium-low and simmer uncovered for 35–45 minutes until the lentils are tender and fully cooked. Make sure the lentils have softened completely and break apart when gently squeezed between your fingers. If they haven't cooked through at this stage, they won't break down further once the remaining ingredients are added.

3. Once the gram has cooked, heat the oil or ghee in a large pan over a medium heat. Add the cumin seeds and cook for a minute until they begin to crackle. Add the chillies and asafoetida, and cook for a further minute.

4. Add the onions and cook until deep golden, about 6–8 minutes. Add the ginger and garlic pastes and cook for a minute, then add the chilli powder and ground coriander. Cook the spices for a minute, then add the tomatoes and cook until the oil separates to the top, about 5–7 minutes.

5. Now add the cooked gram to the pan and mix well. Bring the mixture to a gentle boil, then reduce the heat and add the garam masala and salt. Add 400–500ml of water and simmer for 5–10 minutes, stirring occasionally and mashing some of the gram with the back of the spoon each time you stir. Mashing helps thicken the dish. Check the seasoning and adjust if necessary.

6. Garnish with freshly chopped coriander leaves and serve with wedges of lime or lemon.

Mum's Sambhar-style Dal

**Serves 4 as a main or
6 as a side**

*****

200g raw yellow pigeon
  pea lentils

1 tsp ground turmeric

2 tbsp neutral oil

1 tsp black mustard seeds

½ tsp fenugreek seeds

½ tsp asafoetida

150g onions, finely sliced

8–10 curry leaves

150g potatoes, peeled and cut
  into 2.5cm cubes

1 medium carrot (about
  100–150g), peeled and cut into
  2.5cm cubes

1 small aubergine (about 150g),
  cut into 2.5cm cubes

4 tsp store-bought sambhar
  powder

2 tsp salt, or to taste

2 tsp tamarind paste

100g fresh tomatoes, cut into
  2.5cm cubes

Sambhar is a lentil and vegetable stew traditionally served with idlis and dosas. Different regions and communities have their own variations of this dish. Growing up, Mum always made our sambhar thicker than the traditional version. What I love about her version is that it both serves as a great dip for idlis and Dosas (page 40), and is equally delicious and wholesome by itself, served on plain rice. Load it up with vegetables and you've got a wonderful, quick and easy weeknight supper.

1. Wash the lentils thoroughly in several changes of water until the water runs somewhat clear, then soak in fresh water for 2–3 hours.

2. Put the soaked and drained lentils into a large pot with half the turmeric and 1.5 litres of water. Bring to the boil, then reduce the heat to medium-low and simmer uncovered for 35–45 minutes until the lentils are tender and fully cooked. Make sure the lentils have softened completely and break apart when gently squeezed between your fingers. If they don't break apart, continue boiling them until they do. Once cooked, mash about half of them with the back of a spoon.

3. While the lentils are cooking, heat the oil in a deep pan set over a medium heat and add the mustard seeds and fenugreek seeds. Once the mustard seeds begin to crackle, add the asafoetida, onions and curry leaves. Cook for 3 minutes, or until the onions become translucent and soften slightly – they don't need to go deep brown.

4. Add the potatoes, carrot and aubergine, along with 500ml of water or enough to cover them. Add the remaining turmeric, sambhar powder and salt. Bring to the boil, then reduce the heat and simmer for 10–12 minutes until the vegetables are tender but continue to hold their shape.

5. Add the boiled lentils and any cooking liquid to the vegetables, along with the tamarind paste and tomatoes. Bring it all to the boil, then reduce the heat and cook for 20 minutes. Once you have achieved your desired consistency, check the seasoning, adding more salt or tamarind to your taste. Cook for a further 2–3 minutes.

6. Serve hot.

Eggs

AND

DAIRY

Masala Beans and Eggs on Toast

Serves 2 as a light meal

*****

For the masala baked beans

1 tbsp neutral oil

½ tsp black mustard seeds

50g onion, finely chopped

2 garlic cloves, grated

2.5cm ginger, grated

1 green chilli, finely chopped

8–10 curry leaves

1½ tsp Madras curry powder

½ tsp ground turmeric

½ tsp Kashmiri red chilli powder

1 x 400g tin of baked beans

salt, to taste

*****

For the toast and eggs

1 tbsp butter or neutral oil, for frying the eggs

2 thick slices of sourdough bread

2 large eggs

*****

For the chilli oil tarka

1 tbsp butter or neutral oil

1 tsp cumin seeds

5–6 curry leaves, finely chopped

1 tsp Kashmiri red chilli powder

Tinned baked beans were a novelty for us when we were growing up, and we'd occasionally have them as part of a 'continental' brunch. However, they were rarely served straight from the tin; instead, they were spiced up with curry leaves, mustard seeds, garlic and a whole load of masalas.

As a student in the UK, I developed multiple versions of this dish based on the time and ingredients I had available. Even today, we cook masala beans at least once a week, typically at weekends.

This fully loaded version is perfect for brunch, a light meal, or even a late-night snack. For a touch of indulgence, add a slice of cheese under the piping hot beans. Or for a lighter option, skip the eggs. Most importantly, feel free to experiment and create your own signature version of this very versatile dish.

1. Heat the oil in a pan over a medium heat, then add the mustard seeds and let them crackle. Add the onion with a pinch of salt and cook until soft and translucent, about 2–3 minutes. Add the garlic, ginger, green chilli and curry leaves and cook for another 2–3 minutes, then stir in the curry powder, turmeric and chilli powder. Cook for a minute, then add the baked beans to the pan, stirring to combine. Add a splash of water and simmer for 3–4 minutes until fully heated through. Add salt to taste.

2. While the beans are simmering, heat 1 tablespoon of butter in another pan over a medium heat. Once foaming, place the slices of bread in the pan and fry on both sides until golden, adding more butter if required. Transfer the toasts to serving plates and top with the beans.

3. In the same pan, fry your eggs sunny side up until the whites are set but the yolks are still runny. Place the eggs on top of the beans.

4. For the chilli oil tarka, heat another tablespoon of butter or oil in the pan. Add the cumin seeds and curry leaves and, once the seeds crackle, take the pan off the heat. Add the chilli powder to the hot butter or oil and mix thoroughly, cooking the chilli in the residual heat for 30 seconds. Spoon over the eggs and serve immediately.

Parsi Eggs on Potatoes

Serves 3–4 as a light meal

*****

500g potatoes, peeled and cut
  into 3–4mm slices

3 tbsp neutral oil

200g onions, thinly sliced

¾ tsp ground turmeric

2 green chillies, finely chopped

3–4 eggs

50g fresh ripe tomatoes,
  finely chopped

salt and pepper

2 tbsp finely chopped fresh
  coriander leaves, to garnish

We cook this dish at home as a quick weekend brunch or an early supper on Sunday nights. Its simplicity is a true reflection of Parsi cuisine – practical, unpretentious, yet incredibly flavourful. Bringing together potatoes and eggs with a handful of other ingredients, all cooked in a single pan, it rivals the Spanish with their frittata. I love piling a slice of it onto heavily buttered toast, though it's just as satisfying eaten on its own.

1. Soak the potatoes in salted water for 5–10 minutes, then drain and wipe them dry with a clean towel before cooking.

2. Heat the oil in a non-stick pan over a medium heat. Add the onions along with ½ teaspoon of salt and cook for 3–5 minutes until soft and translucent.

3. Add the turmeric, green chillies, potatoes and another ½ teaspoon of salt and cook over a medium-high heat for 2–3 minutes, then reduce the heat to low, cover and cook for 8–10 minutes until the potatoes have fully cooked through, but are not mushy.

4. Once the potatoes have cooked, spread them out evenly in the pan and use the bottom of an egg to make three or four shallow dents in them. Crack an egg into each dent and sprinkle some salt and pepper over each. Sprinkle over the chopped tomatoes, cover the pan and cook for 3–4 minutes until the egg whites are set but the yolks are still runny. If you prefer firmer yolks, cook for a few minutes longer.

5. Garnish with freshly chopped coriander and serve hot, with generously buttered toast.

Ros
Omelette

Serves 2 as a main

*****

For the gravy

2 tbsp neutral oil

¾ tsp cumin seeds

200g onions, finely chopped

1 tsp garlic paste

1 tsp ginger paste

2 green chillies, slit lengthways

½ tsp ground turmeric

1 tsp ground coriander

1½ tsp garam masala (see
    page 267 for homemade)

1 tbsp red chilli paste
    (see page 15)

150g fresh ripe tomatoes,
    finely chopped (or 120g
    tinned tomatoes)

300ml coconut milk

150–200ml chicken or
    vegetable stock

½ tsp sugar

1 tsp salt, to taste

*****

For the omelette

4 eggs

50g red onions, finely chopped

1 green chilli, finely chopped

50g fresh ripe tomatoes,
    finely chopped

2 tbsp finely chopped fresh
    coriander leaves

½ tsp salt, to taste

2 tbsp neutral oil or butter

*****

To serve

30g red onion, finely chopped

1 tbsp finely chopped fresh
    coriander leaves

2 lime wedges

A favourite late-night street food in Goa, this dish is a glorious combination of a masala omelette bathed in a spicy ros (gravy). The gravy also serves as a great base for a boiled egg or prawn curry, if you want to switch it up. Traditionally, this dish is eaten with Goan poie, a fluffy bran bread similar to wholewheat pitta bread, or pillowy pav buns. However, I often enjoy this as a quick weeknight supper with thick-cut sliced white bread.

1. Start with the gravy. Heat the oil in a large pan over a medium heat, then add the cumin seeds and let them crackle. Add the onions and cook until they turn golden brown, about 7–8 minutes, then add the garlic and ginger pastes and green chillies and cook for 2–3 minutes until fragrant.

2. Stir in the turmeric, ground coriander and garam masala and cook for 30 seconds, adding water if the spices begin to stick to the pan.

3. Add the red chilli paste and chopped tomatoes and cook until the oil begins to separate and come to the surface, about 6–8 minutes.

4. Pour in the coconut milk along with the chicken or vegetable stock, and add sugar and salt to taste. Bring to the boil, then reduce the heat and let it simmer for 10–12 minutes until it thickens. To achieve the traditional smooth texture of this dish, you can blend the gravy and pass it through a fine sieve at this stage. However, I often leave it chunky. Once ready, set aside while you prepare the omelette. The gravy can be made up to two days in advance and heated up just before serving.

5. For the omelette, beat the eggs thoroughly in a mixing bowl. Add the onions, chilli, tomatoes, coriander leaves and salt, and mix well.

6. Heat a tablespoon of oil or butter in a non-stick pan over a medium heat and pour in half the egg mix to form a flat omelette. Cook until the edges are golden and the centre is set, about 2 minutes, then flip over for a further minute. Roll the omelette and transfer it to a serving plate.

7. Repeat the process with the second half of the egg mix.

8. Once both omelettes are cooked, ladle the hot curry over them. Garnish with finely chopped red onion, fresh coriander leaves and a wedge of lime, and serve hot.

Egg Curry

Serves 2 as a light meal

*****

4 eggs, fridge-cold

1½ tbsp coconut oil

½ tsp black mustard seeds

3–4 green cardamom pods

½ tsp fennel seeds

1 tsp grated ginger

1 tsp grated garlic

1 green chilli, slit in half
   lengthways

160g onions, finely chopped

10–12 curry leaves

1½ tsp salt

1 tbsp ground coriander

1 tsp Kashmiri red chilli powder

½ tsp ground turmeric

200g ripe fresh tomatoes, finely
   chopped (or 130g tinned
   chopped tomatoes)

150ml coconut milk

chilli oil, to garnish

Growing up in a predominantly vegetarian home in India, an egg curry was the closest my mum would get to cooking 'non-vegetarian' food at home. Over the years and many egg curries later, I lost my excitement for the dish, until one day I tried a version my Keralan chef Renjith cooked for a staff meal at Hoppers. This is his recipe – one he tells me he cooks for his family every weekend. It's the perfect dish for a quick weeknight supper or weekend brunch, along with some plain rice or Malabar Parottas (page 212) to scoop up the curry.

Traditionally, eggs are hard-boiled before they are added to curries, but I choose a soft jellied yolk over a powdery dry one any day and in any dish. The recipe below yields a soft egg, but feel free to boil yours for 8 minutes if you prefer the traditional version.

1. Bring a large pan of water to the boil and add the eggs very carefully, making sure they don't bounce and crack. Once the water returns to the boil, set a timer for 5½ minutes. When the timer goes off, remove the eggs and plunge them into cold water to stop them cooking. Peel and set aside. You could do this ahead and keep the eggs in the fridge.

2. Heat the coconut oil in a pan over a medium heat. Add the mustard seeds and, once they crackle, add the cardamom pods, fennel seeds, ginger, garlic, green chilli, onions and curry leaves with ½ teaspoon of salt. Cook for 6–8 minutes, stirring occasionally, until the onions turn golden.

3. Add the remaining spices and cook for a further 30 seconds.

4. Add the tomatoes and cook until everything has come together into a thick sauce, about 6–8 minutes. Add 200–250ml of water and continue simmering for a couple of minutes.

5. Add the coconut milk and remaining 1 teaspoon of salt and simmer for a couple of minutes until you have a beautiful, rich curry.

6. When ready to eat, add the eggs to the simmering curry and cook for 2–3 minutes. Serve immediately, drizzled with chilli oil.

Dairy

Ghee, yoghurt (aka curd) and paneer have a vital place in Indian culture. Cooking aside, these items are also offered to gods in various traditional Hindu rituals, and ghee holds a special place in Ayurveda or Indian medicine. No Indian festival is complete without consuming large amounts of dairy, in one form or another – ghee, paneer or desserts like gulab jamuns, barfis, rasgullas, kheer, payasam and so on.

While references to dairy have been found in ancient texts, it wasn't until the 1970s and the advent of collective farming (or cooperative farming, as it's known in India) that India's dairy farming grew exponentially. Today, India is the world's largest milk producer, with nearly double the output of the USA, which sits in second place. Amul, India's largest dairy collective, spearheaded the dairy movement and still manufactures some of India's most beloved dairy products – Amul butter and cheese. When I was growing up in Mumbai, I eagerly waited for friends and family travelling abroad to bring home Kraft singles and Laughing Cow wedges, but nowadays I never return from India without a stash of Amul cheese!

The dairy recipes in this chapter can easily be bought from stores or large supermarkets, but I'd encourage you to try making some. There's a unique satisfaction and sheer joy in making these basic provisions – things you are so used to being made in factories – in your home kitchen. And if, like me, you grew up in an Indian household, making these will also give you a deep sense of nostalgia.

So, if time allows, do try making some of these dairy staples yourself. They'll (hopefully) taste better and give you something to brag about to friends and family when they come by for supper.

Paneer

Makes 175–200g

*****

1 litre full-fat milk (I use gold top
    milk in the UK and buffalo's milk
    in India)

juice of ½ lemon, or as needed

2 tbsp Greek-style yoghurt

½ tsp fine salt, or more to taste

2 tbsp mixed herbs and spices
    of your choice – I use ground
    cumin, pepper and fresh
    coriander (optional)

Paneer originates in northern India, but today you'll struggle to find a menu anywhere in the country that doesn't have paneer on it. It's a favourite in everything from snacks to curries and stir-fries, and vegetarians across the nation view it as a vital source of protein and calcium.

Unlike many cheeses, which need specialist tools and enzymes, paneer is ridiculously quick and easy to make at home. I add spices and herbs to my paneer to take it up to the next level – especially when simply pan-frying it in some ghee or brown butter – but you're welcome to leave these out for a more traditional, plain version.

1. Boil the milk over a medium heat, stirring constantly so it doesn't form a skin on the surface or stick to the pan. Take it off the heat once it has boiled for 2 minutes.

2. Mix the lemon juice and yoghurt and tip it into the boiled milk. Stir and leave aside for 3–4 minutes. The milk will split and the whey should be a clear greenish colour. If it's still cloudy, add a little more lemon juice and warm it gently until clear.

3. When the milk has fully split, add a few cubes of ice, as this stops the curds overcooking and keeps the paneer soft.

4. Strain everything through a sieve lined with a clean tea towel or muslin cloth. Set aside the liquid (whey) and wash the curds (solid white bits) gently in running water to remove any remaining sour flavour. Add the salt, herbs and spices (if using) to the curds and mix well.

5. Wrap the curds tightly into a parcel and sandwich between two flat surfaces (I place it on a chopping board and balance a heavy pan on top). The paneer should be ready to unwrap and use in about 30 minutes.

Notes

- Homemade paneer can be crumblier than store-bought versions. To prevent it breaking up in your gravy, lightly pan-fry it before adding it to a curry. If, however, you are using store-bought paneer and find it's not soft enough when added to a gravy or stir-fry, try soaking it in slightly salted boiling water for 5 minutes before drying it thoroughly and using it as per the recipe.
- The leftover whey from paneer-making is packed with protein and is really healthy. Mix it into bread doughs, curries, smoothies, or drink it as is. You can even water plants with it.
- Paneer can be frozen. Thaw it in the fridge overnight, and pop it into boiling water for 5 minutes before drying and using it.

Ghee

Makes about 400g

*****

500g good-quality
   unsalted butter

Ghee is naively referred to as clarified butter, but good ghee is so much more! It's used to pan-fry, deep-fry and garnish a whole host of dishes ranging from curries to tarkas, and desserts to deep-fried snacks. In my homemade version I like browning the milk fats until they get nutty, giving the ghee a delicious caramelized flavour. This recipe is dead easy and needs just a single ingredient and some patience.

1. Place the butter in a heavy-bottomed pan over a medium heat and bring to a gentle simmer once it melts.

2. Keep the butter simmering gently (110–115°C to be precise, if you have a probe). You'll begin to hear a popping sound as drops of water turn to vapour and evaporate. This will go on for about 15–20 minutes. Don't stir the bottom, and there's no need to skim off the froth, as these are the milk solids that will settle and caramelize later, giving the ghee that beautiful nutty flavour.

3. Once the popping reduces, increase the heat slightly (to 125–130°C if you're still measuring) and cook until the milk solids sink to the bottom of the pan and go brown and smell like caramel. You will need to watch the pan like a hawk at this stage, because it can go from beautiful nutty to burnt acrid in a few seconds.

4. Once you're happy with the flavour and caramelization, pull the pan off the heat and strain the golden liquid through a sieve lined with a clean tea towel or muslin cloth. You can discard the brown solids or use them in desserts or pancakes.

5. Store the ghee in a clean jar. It will set eventually when cool, but can be melted in seconds in a microwave or by placing near a warm hob.

Notes

- Pure ghee has a high smoking point, making it very versatile and a lot healthier than many other processed fats. I use ghee in a lot of Western cooking too. Give it a go when pan-frying fish, roasting chicken or making crêpes and pancakes.
- If made properly, ghee has a long shelf life and doesn't require refrigeration. When stored in an airtight container, it can last for several months without spoiling, due to its low moisture content.

Yoghurt

Makes 1 litre

*****

1 litre full-fat milk

15g live yoghurt

Like making ghee, this recipe requires very little apart from good milk and patience. Yes, if it's the first time you're making it, then you'll also need some starter – nothing too complex, just a tablespoon or two of live yoghurt from a friend or a trusted store-bought source.

Homemade yoghurt is often tastier and a lot healthier than store-bought alternatives, which frequently contain stabilizers, sugar and preservatives.

1. Pour the milk into a heavy-bottomed pan over a low heat and bring to a simmer.

2. Continue simmering the milk for 15 minutes, stirring occasionally. Then sit the pan in a tray filled with cold water to cool the milk down rapidly.

3. Once the milk has reduced to about 46°C, add the yoghurt and stir thoroughly. Pour into a glass, stainless-steel or earthenware bowl, cover with clingfilm or foil, and wrap a thick tea towel round it to keep it warm. Leave it wrapped in a cupboard or switched-off oven for 8–10 hours.

4. Eat immediately, or keep chilled in the fridge for up to a week. For a thicker, Greek-style version, leave the yoghurt in a fine mesh sieve lined with a muslin cloth for 4–6 hours in the fridge to let it strain thoroughly.

Troubleshooting Tips

- Runny yoghurt can be the result of using low-fat milk or poor live cultures. Try giving the cultures a little longer to incubate, or use a different starter yoghurt next time. Yoghurt can also fail to set if it is too cold.
- Sour yoghurt is often the result of over-incubation or too much starter yoghurt. Reduce the time or starter the next time. And don't bin the sour yoghurt, you can use it to make a delicious Gujarati Kadhi (page 102).
- Watery whey separation can occur if the yoghurt is disturbed during the incubation process. Avoid shaking or drastic temperature changes while the yoghurt sets.

Palak Paneer

Serves 4 as a main

*****

250g paneer, cut into batons

1½ tbsp ghee

1 tsp cumin seeds

120g red onions, finely chopped

1½ tsp salt, to taste

1 tsp grated ginger

½ tsp grated garlic

100g fresh ripe tomatoes,
   finely chopped (or 80g tinned
   chopped tomatoes)

½ tsp kasoori methi (dried
   fenugreek leaves) (optional)

250g spinach leaves

1 green chilli, slit in half
   lengthways

1 tbsp fresh cream, to garnish

5cm ginger, peeled and cut into
   matchsticks, to garnish

Outside of India, any green, mostly spinach-based Indian sauce is naively referred to as 'saag'. This is like calling any type of pie just a 'pie', despite the differences between a shepherd's pie and a steak and ale pie. In India, saag refers to a variety of leafy greens, used in numerous dishes ranging from mustard greens (sarson) to fenugreek (methi) and beyond. This recipe from north India uses spinach (palak) as the main ingredient and is the version I grew up eating at home the most.

It's one of the simplest recipes in the book, very healthy, and a family favourite, so it's ideal to batch cook. Serve alongside some Fulkas (page 208) or Parathas (page 216).

1. If you're using store-bought paneer you can cut and soak it in a bowl of boiling water while you prepare the gravy. Soaking the paneer helps to make it a lot softer when cooked. If you're using homemade paneer you can pan-fry it until golden brown before adding it to the curry, especially if it is quite crumbly.

2. Heat the ghee in a pan over a medium heat and add the cumin seeds. Once they crackle, tip in the red onions along with ½ teaspoon of salt. When the onions have softened, after about 3 minutes, add the ginger and garlic and cook for another 2 minutes.

3. Now add the tomatoes and kasoori methi (if using) and cook for about 3–4 minutes, until the tomatoes have reduced by a third, adding a splash of water if required.

4. Wash and add the spinach, then cover the pan. Some cooks boil the spinach and then add it, but I prefer adding it fresh and preserving all the juices and nutrients. Cook the spinach until it just wilts in its own steam and juices, about 3 minutes. Take the pan off the heat and blitz everything, along with 1 teaspoon of salt, the green chilli and 100ml of water.

5. Once you have a smooth sauce, return it to the pan. Bring it back to a simmer and check the seasoning and consistency, adding water if you like it thinner.

6. Add the paneer and cook for 3–4 minutes, until fully warmed through. Garnish with a drizzle of cream and the ginger before serving.

Chilli Paneer

**Serves 2 as a main or
4 as a starter or side**

*****

400g paneer, cubed

1½ tsp salt, to taste

½ tsp ground turmeric

1½ tsp Kashmiri red chilli powder

4–5 tbsp neutral oil

100g red onions, cubed

150g red or green peppers, cubed

1 tsp grated ginger

2 tsp grated garlic

10–12 curry leaves

2 green chillies, slit lengthways

2 tbsp tomato ketchup

2 tsp dark soy sauce

1 tsp white vinegar (rice vinegar or
white wine vinegar)

a pinch of MSG (see page 256)
(optional)

1 tbsp cornflour, mixed with
200ml water

a handful of chopped spring
onions, to garnish

Indo-Chinese cuisine could easily be considered a sub-cuisine of India, given its wide range of innovative dishes and omnipresence across the country. Kolkata, Mumbai and Kochi (among other cities and towns) all have their versions of Indo-Chinese dishes, which usually feature soy, vinegar, chillies, spices and a copious amount of ginger and garlic. If you're new to this genre, this recipe is a great starting point. It's a dish that's found everywhere, from streetside carts to fancy restaurants. My version has a south Indian touch to it with the addition of curry leaves. I love them in most things, but you can leave them out if you can't find them.

This is a great starter but can also be served as a main alongside fried rice or noodles.

1. Soak the paneer in boiling water for 15 minutes, then drain and sprinkle over ½ teaspoon each of salt, turmeric and chilli powder. Mix well.

2. Heat the oil in a wok over a medium-high heat and fry the paneer, turning it until lightly coloured on all sides, 3–4 minutes. You might need to do this in batches if your wok is small. Remove with a slotted spoon to a sieve or some kitchen paper to drain any excess oil. Alternatively, you could deep-fry the paneer in a 5cm depth of oil for 2–3 minutes, or brush or spray a little oil over the paneer and air-fry it for 6–8 minutes on high.

3. In the same wok, fry the onions and green peppers for 30 seconds. You want to get them glossy, retaining their shape and crunch, without them getting overcooked and limp. Remember they will be cooked briefly in the sauce later. Remove the vegetables and set aside with the paneer.

4. Leave about 1 teaspoon of oil in the pan and reduce the heat to medium. Add the ginger and garlic and cook for a minute or two until golden and aromatic, being careful not to let them burn. Add the remaining chilli powder, curry leaves, green chillies, tomato ketchup, soy sauce, vinegar and MSG (if using) and cook for about 2 minutes, then add the cornflour mixture. Continue cooking for 4–5 minutes, stirring constantly until the sauce is thick and glossy.

5. Add the onions, peppers and paneer to the sauce with a teaspoon of salt, or to taste, and cook for a further 2–3 minutes.

6. Garnish with spring onions and serve.

Paneer Shashlik

Serves 2 as a main or

4 as a snack or starter

*****

800g paneer, cut into 2.5cm
squares about 1cm in thickness

2 medium red onions, cut into
2.5cm pieces

4 tomatoes, seeds removed and
cut into 5cm pieces

1 green pepper, seeds removed
and cut into 2.5cm pieces

metal or wooden skewers
(if using wooden skewers,
soak in water for 30 minutes to
prevent burning)

melted butter or oil, for basting

For the marinade

1 tsp each ginger and garlic paste

1 tsp kasoori methi (dried
fenugreek leaves)

½ tsp ground turmeric

1 tsp garam masala (see page 267
for homemade)

½ tsp carom seeds (optional)

¼ tsp black peppercorns, crushed

200g Greek-style yoghurt

2 tbsp mustard oil

1½ tsp salt

To garnish

1 tbsp melted butter

1 tsp chaat masala (see page 266
for homemade)

2 tbsp finely chopped fresh
coriander

1 green chilli, finely chopped

I remember skipping classes at university to go eat at Kobe, a buzzing restaurant in Mumbai famous for its sizzlers. These dishes were a feast in themselves, featuring rice, crispy chips, grilled meat or paneer, and a medley of vegetables, all served on a sizzling hot plate with a selection of irresistible sauces to pour. Years later, I found myself reunited with this dish at a neighbourhood Indian restaurant in London, where they served their paneer tikka on a sizzling plate and called it paneer shashlik, just like Kobe.

There's something about the sizzler experience – the dramatic smoke, the enticing aroma, the crackling sound, and the sheer theatre of it all as it arrives at your table – that elevates the flavour of grilled proteins. If you happen to have a sizzler plate or thick cast-iron pan to serve this on, go ahead and replicate the drama in your home. But even without the theatrics, you're going to fall in love with this dish. If you are going for it, heat your pan on the highest setting on the hob. Then, just before serving the paneer, add some sliced onions to the pan. They should sizzle fiercely, creating a lovely bed for the paneer to rest on and preventing it from burning. Finish with a generous drizzle of melted butter to produce that signature plume of smoke as you carry the dish over to the table.

1. Mix all the ingredients for the marinade in a large mixing bowl and coat the paneer and vegetable pieces in it. Cover and refrigerate for 30 minutes.

2. Prepare the skewers – start with a piece of paneer, followed by a piece of onion, tomato and green pepper, and repeat until the skewer is full. Repeat with the remaining skewers.

3. *If cooking in the oven:* Preheat the grill to high and place a tray lined with foil on the middle shelf. Once the tray is hot, place the paneer skewers on it and grill for 8–10 minutes, turning halfway and basting with melted butter. If the paneer hasn't charred in spots after 8 minutes, move the tray to the top shelf and continue to cook directly under the grill for 2–5 minutes, turning the skewers every couple of minutes.

If cooking on the stove: Heat a heavy pan over a medium-high heat. Melt a teaspoon of butter in the pan and when it starts to brown, add the paneer skewers and cook for 8–10 minutes, cooking constantly to ensure they colour evenly on all sides.

If cooking on the barbecue: Place the skewers on a well-oiled rack directly over the flames and cook for 8–10 minutes, turning every couple of minutes. Make sure the rack is very hot before placing the skewers on it, to avoid them sticking. The exact cooking time will depend on the height of the rack and the temperature.

4. Drizzle the paneer skewers with melted butter and sprinkle over the chaat masala, fresh coriander and green chilli before serving.

Gujarati Kadhi

**Serves 4 as a main or
6 as a side**

*****

4 tbsp gram flour

300g natural yoghurt

5cm ginger, grated

1½ tsp salt

1–2 tsp jaggery, or granulated
sugar

1 tbsp chopped fresh coriander
leaves

*****

For the spiced oil

1½ tbsp ghee or neutral oil

1 tsp cumin seeds

½ tsp fenugreek seeds

2 dried red chillies, stems and
seeds removed

12–15 curry leaves

½ tsp asafoetida

5 cloves

5cm cinnamon stick

Growing up in India I don't remember hearing the word 'curry'. Common belief is that the word comes from the Tamil word 'kari'. Sadly, I don't speak the language and didn't grow up anywhere close to Tamil Nadu. However, kadhi (pronounced cud-hee) is a very popular dish made with yoghurt in the west and north, and was the closest we ever got to the ubiquitous English term that seems to describe most Indian dishes today.

Jargon aside, you'll rarely eat a Gujarati meal without a kadhi featuring in one form or another. As with most Gujarati food, this dish can be quite sweet, so reduce the amount of jaggery or sugar if you prefer a more savoury version. I love it sweet, and, in fact, one of my favourite variations of the Gujarati kadhi is made with mangoes. If you've got some fresh or tinned mango pulp to hand, replace 100g of the yoghurt with mango pulp, and add it at step 3 in the last 5 minutes of simmering the kadhi. Enjoy it with some rice or piping hot Puris (page 220) to dip in.

1. In a large bowl, whisk together the gram flour with 200ml of water until there are no lumps, then add 500ml more water, the yoghurt, ginger, salt and jaggery and continue whisking till smooth. Set aside.

2. For the spiced oil, heat the ghee or oil in a large pan over a medium heat. Add the cumin seeds, fenugreek seeds, dried red chillies, curry leaves, asafoetida, cloves and cinnamon, and cook for 30 seconds until fragrant.

3. Take the pan off the heat and pour in the yoghurt mixture, stirring continuously to prevent curdling. Return to a medium heat and bring the mixture to a gentle simmer, then reduce the heat to low and cook for about 20 minutes, stirring occasionally, until the kadhi thickens. Add more water if you prefer the kadhi thinner.

4. Check the seasoning and adjust if necessary. Stir in the coriander leaves and serve hot.

FISH

and

SHELL FISH

Salmon Tikka

**Serves 2 as a main or
4 as a starter or snack**

*****

600–800g salmon fillet, cut into
4 equal pieces

*****

For the marinade

1 tsp each ginger and garlic paste

1 tsp crushed kasoori methi (dried
fenugreek leaves)

½ tsp ground turmeric

½ tsp fennel seeds

½ tsp garam masala (see
page 267 for homemade)

¼ tsp crushed black peppercorns

2 tbsp Greek-style yoghurt

1 egg white (optional)

2 tbsp cream cheese

1 green chilli, finely chopped

6 green cardamom pods, seeds
crushed to a powder

2 tbsp melted butter, plus more
to garnish

1 tsp salt

*****

To garnish

1 tsp chaat masala (see page 266
for homemade)

a few dill leaves

Salmon isn't a fish that you typically find in Indian waters, as it is native
to colder climates. However, Indian restaurants across the UK have been
serving variations of tandoori salmon for years, and it's now a regular on
menus. The spiced yoghurt marinade pairs exceptionally well with salmon,
while the natural fattiness of the fish ensures that it remains moist and
juicy when cooked over a high heat, such as a grill or in a tandoor.

If you're preparing this dish in a region where salmon isn't readily
available, you can easily substitute it with any local oily fish. Fish like
trout, halibut, sea bass, bream, snapper, barramundi and Arctic char
work wonderfully.

Serve alongside a Kachumber salad (page 176) or Raita (page 173) and
some Lemon Rice (page 192) or Tamarind Rice (page 195) for a glorious
supper on a spring or summer evening.

1. Mix all the ingredients for the marinade in a large mixing bowl and coat
the salmon pieces in it. Cover and refrigerate for 30 minutes.

2. Barbecue the salmon pieces or place in a roasting tray and bake at
200–220°C fan for 12–15 minutes until charred in spots but still pink in
the middle. If the salmon has not got spots of char after this time,
switch the oven to grill mode on the maximum setting and place the
tray on the top shelf for a further minute or two.

3. Drizzle the salmon with melted butter and sprinkle over the chaat
masala and dill leaves before serving.

Prawn Balchao

Serves 2 as a main

*****

3 tbsp neutral oil

10–12 curry leaves

500g onions, finely chopped

1 tsp salt, or to taste

1 tsp ginger paste

2 tsp garlic paste

½ tsp ground turmeric

2 green chillies, slit lengthways

500g prawns, cleaned
   and deveined

1 tbsp sugar

*****

For the masala paste

6 cloves

2.5cm cinnamon stick

1 tsp black peppercorns

1 tsp cumin seeds

1 tbsp coriander seeds

6–8 Kashmiri red chillies, stems
   and seeds removed

2 tsp dried shrimp (optional)

150ml apple cider vinegar or white
   wine vinegar, to taste

This versatile Goan prawn dish can be served as either the star of the meal or as a punchy pickle on the side. Traditionally, it was made as a pickle, with vinegar and spices preserving the prawns so they could be eaten over several days without needing refrigeration. These days, it's a favourite at Goan festivals and special occasions, where it's served as a main dish. It's just as mouthwatering when made with squid, lobster, or crayfish. Serve with plain rice or some crusty white bread.

1. Start by making the masala paste. Heat a small dry pan over a medium heat and toast the cloves, cinnamon, peppercorns, cumin seeds and coriander seeds for 2 minutes until fragrant.

2. Transfer the toasted spices, red chillies and dried shrimp (if using) to a bowl. Pour the vinegar over them and mix well. Let everything soak in the vinegar for 2 hours, or ideally overnight, then blend to a fine paste, adding a little water if needed, and set aside.

3. To make the curry, heat the oil in a pan over a medium heat. Add the curry leaves, followed by the onions and ¼ teaspoon of salt. Cook for 6–8 minutes, until the onions soften and turn light brown.

4. Stir in the ginger, garlic, turmeric, green chillies and the remaining salt and cook until the aromatics turn deep brown, approximately 6–8 minutes, adding a little water from time to time if required.

5. Add the masala paste to the pan and cook over a low heat for 8–10 minutes, until the oil rises to the surface.

6. Add the prawns, mixing well to coat them with the masala, then add 150ml of water and cook for 4–5 minutes. Add the sugar and adjust the seasoning to your taste, adding more salt or vinegar to find your perfect balance.

7. Serve immediately or refrigerate for up to two days. Like many Goan dishes, this continues to mature with time, and I find it tastes better when reheated the next day. Serve hot.

Crispy Semolina Fish Fry

**Serves 4 as a snack
or starter**

*****

500g any small white fish fillets,
such as gurnard, whiting,
kingfish, etc.

oil, to deep-fry

2 tbsp finely chopped fresh
coriander leaves, to serve

1 red onion, cut into rings, to serve

4–6 lime or lemon wedges,
to serve

*****

For the marinade

juice of 1 lime or lemon

½ tsp ground turmeric

1 tsp Kashmiri red chilli powder

½ tsp ginger paste (optional)

½ tsp garlic paste (optional)

½ tsp salt

*****

For the crust

100g coarse semolina

75g rice flour

½ tsp salt

Coarse semolina, or rawa as it's commonly known, is the star of the popular rawa fish fry found across western India, famous for its irresistibly crunchy coating, which locks in all the juiciness of the fish. It's a staple on fish thalis, the delightful set meals found all over Goa and Maharashtra. Depending on the season and location, you might come across a variety of fish prepared this way, from kingfish steaks to pomfret. One of the first things I eat when I land in Mumbai is a freshly fried bombil, also known as Bombay duck (which is in fact a unique, eel-like fish), served with a spicy coriander chutney. If you happen to come across some fresh or frozen bombil (not the dried kind that's more common), I highly recommend trying this recipe with it. It might just become your new favourite fried fish!

1. Mix all the ingredients for the marinade in a bowl, adding a splash of water to form a thin paste. Wipe the fish fillets with kitchen paper to make sure they are completely dry. Rub the marinade all over them and let them rest at room temperature for 15–20 minutes.

2. Mix the semolina, rice flour and salt together in a plate or shallow dish. Take each marinated fillet and lay it in the semolina mixture, pressing lightly to ensure an even coating. Flip to make sure both sides are crusted.

3. I like to deep-fry this fish for best results, but shallow-frying it in a deep frying pan with a generous layer of oil works well too.

If deep-frying: heat oil in a deep pan or wok over a medium-high heat. Once the oil is hot, add the coated fish fillets in batches, making sure not to overcrowd the pan. Fry until golden brown and crispy, about 3–4 minutes per batch. Remove the fried fish pieces with a slotted spoon and drain on kitchen paper. Repeat with the remaining fish.

If shallow-frying: heat 3–4 tablespoons of oil in a large pan over a medium heat. The oil should be hot but not smoking. Gently place the crusted fish fillets in the hot oil and fry for about 2–3 minutes, then carefully flip the fish using a flat spatula to prevent the crust falling off. Cook for another 2–3 minutes, until the coating is golden brown and crisp, and the fish is cooked through. Avoid overcrowding the pan – fry in batches if necessary.

4. Serve the fish hot, garnished with chopped coriander, onion rings and a wedge of lime or lemon.

Prawn Moilee

Serves 2 as a main

*****

For the prawns

250g prawns, heads and shells
   removed and deveined

½ tsp each salt and black pepper

¼ tsp ground turmeric

juice of ½ lime

*****

For the curry

1½ tbsp coconut oil

½ tsp black mustard seeds

½ tsp fenugreek seeds

8–10 curry leaves

160g red onions, thinly sliced

1 tsp ginger paste

1 tsp garlic paste

1½ tsp salt, to taste

½ tsp ground turmeric

400ml coconut milk

2 green chillies, stems removed,
   slit in half lengthways

6–8 cherry tomatoes (optional),
   cut in half

This easy Keralan prawn curry is packed with flavour and is ready in minutes – you'll find yourself making it again and again. It's perfect for a quick weeknight meal, and the sauce is just as delicious with pumpkin, chicken or fish if you want to switch it up. Serve with plain rice or as part of a larger feast.

The recipe is also a great option for those who enjoy delicately spiced Indian food, without heat. It's an inherently mild dish, but you can further dial it down a few notches by adding some extra coconut milk or even skipping the chillies.

1. Mix together the prawns, salt, pepper, turmeric and lime juice and leave to marinate at room temperature for 15–20 minutes.

2. To make the curry, heat the coconut oil in a pan set over a medium heat. Add the mustard seeds and fenugreek seeds. Once the mustard seeds begin to crackle, add the curry leaves, onions, ginger and garlic pastes along with ½ teaspoon of salt to ensure everything cooks evenly. Continue cooking for 5–6 minutes, stirring occasionally.

3. Once the onions have fully softened and are just beginning to change colour, add the turmeric and the coconut milk and cook for a minute, then add the prawns and simmer over a low heat for 8–10 minutes.

4. Add the green chillies, tomatoes (if using) and the remaining 1 teaspoon of salt and cook for a further minute. Add more water if you prefer the curry thinner, and check the seasoning. Serve hot.

Banana Leaf Fish

I absolutely love cooking fish in banana leaves – there's something both primitive and magical about unwrapping a banana leaf parcel at the table to reveal a piece of steaming fish. It's an experience that's exciting whether you're cooking for one or many, and it always leaves dinner guests in awe.

In this section, I've included two of my favourite banana leaf recipes – one from Kerala and another beloved by the Parsi community.

Unless you're lucky enough to find very fresh, tender banana leaves, you'll need to scorch them before use to make sure they're supple enough to wrap the fish. To do this, pass a leaf over an open flame, or briefly press it down on a hot pan using a pad of kitchen paper to protect your fingers, until it becomes glossy and changes colour. You'll notice the leaf's texture will alter immediately, making it much easier to wrap the fish.

If you can't find banana leaves, you can still make both recipes. Wrap the fish first in baking parchment and then in foil to create a tight parcel. Then bake it in the oven for 20–25 minutes at 180°C fan.

Kerala-style Fish in Banana Leaf

Serves 2 as a main

*****

600–800g whole fish, ideally bream or mackerel, gutted and cleaned

1 large banana leaf, to wrap the fish

1 tbsp coconut oil

lime or lemon wedges, to serve

*****

For the marinade:

1 tsp Kashmiri red chilli powder

½ tsp ground turmeric

½ tsp ground black pepper

juice of ½ lime or lemon

½ tsp salt

*****

For the masala

2 tbsp coconut oil

8–10 curry leaves

100g onions, finely chopped

1 tsp garlic paste

1 tsp ginger paste

1 green chilli, finely chopped

1 tsp Kashmiri red chilli powder

200g fresh ripe tomatoes (or 150g tinned chopped tomatoes)

100ml coconut milk

½ tsp salt

This delicacy from Kerala is usually made with pearl spot, a river fish locals are so crazy about that it's rarely exported. I've made this with everything from mackerel to sea bream. To cook this quickly on weeknights, prepare a large batch of the flavour-packed onion, tomato and chilli masala and freeze it in portions, so you can defrost some and prepare your fish in minutes. Serve with plain rice or Lemon Rice (page 192). *Pictured overleaf.*

1. Mix all the marinade ingredients in a bowl, adding a splash of water to form a thick paste. Make slits in the fish to allow the marinade to penetrate, then coat it in the marinade and leave to rest for 15–20 minutes.

2. For the masala, heat the coconut oil in a large pan over a medium heat. Add the curry leaves and onions and cook for about 4–5 minutes until the onions soften and turn translucent. Add the garlic and ginger pastes and green chilli and cook for another 2 minutes, then add the chilli powder and cook for another minute. Add the tomatoes and cook for 8–10 minutes until thick and concentrated, adding a splash of water if needed.

3. Once the tomatoes have cooked to a thick paste, pour in the coconut milk, mixing well to combine, and bring to a gentle simmer. Cook for 2–3 minutes until the paste thickens. Allow to cool completely. This paste can be made up to two days ahead of cooking the fish.

4. Preheat the oven to 180°C fan and warm a large banana leaf to make it flexible (see opposite). Spread a thin layer of the masala paste on the leaf, place the fish on top, and generously coat it with more paste. Wrap the fish carefully in the banana leaf.

5. Wipe the pan clean and heat the tablespoon of coconut oil over a medium heat. Add the banana leaf parcel to the pan and fry for 4 minutes on each side, then remove it from the pan and wrap it in foil.

6. Transfer the foil-wrapped parcel to the oven and bake for 10 minutes. Check if the fish is done by piercing it with a sharp knife. The flesh should be fully opaque and should come off the bone easily. The exact cooking time may vary depending on the size of your fish.

7. Unwrap and discard the foil before serving the fish, but leave it wrapped in the banana leaf. Serve with a wedge of lime or lemon on the side.

Parsi-style Fish in Banana Leaf

Serves 2 as a main

*****

600–800g whole fish, ideally
  bream or mackerel, gutted
  and cleaned

1 large banana leaf, to wrap
  the fish

2–3 lime or lemon wedges,
  to serve

*****

For the marinade

½ tsp ground turmeric

½ tsp ground black pepper

juice of ½ lime or lemon

½ tsp salt

*****

For the chutney

50g fresh coriander leaves
  and stems

20g fresh mint leaves

2 green chillies

2 garlic cloves, peeled

1 tsp ginger paste

½ tsp cumin seeds

1½ tsp sugar

50g grated coconut, or 40g
  desiccated coconut, soaked
  for 10 minutes in hot water and
  squeezed dry

50ml chilled water

½ tsp salt, to taste

When we were growing up, we often made this Parsi favourite with silver pomfret, but hake, cod, halibut, and other types of meaty white fish work just as well. The fish is generously covered with a fresh and vibrant coriander, coconut and green chilli chutney, before being wrapped and steamed in fresh banana leaves. Feel free to adapt the green chutney to your taste by adding different herbs or adjusting the quantities of those listed. Serve with a Kachumber salad (page 176) and some rice on the side.

1. Mix all the ingredients for the marinade in a bowl, adding a splash of water to form a thin paste. Make slits in the fish to allow the marinade to penetrate. Coat the fish with the marinade and let it rest for 15–20 minutes.

2. To make the chutney, place all the ingredients in a blender jar and blend to a vibrant green chutney. Using chilled water keeps the chutney bright green. The final texture of the chutney should be smooth and thick enough to coat the fish.

3. To cook the fish, warm a large banana leaf to make it flexible (see page 114). Spread a thin layer of chutney on the leaf, place the fish on top, and generously coat it with more chutney. Wrap the fish carefully in the banana leaf and place it seam-side down on a heatproof plate to prevent it unravelling.

4. Steam the fish for 16–20 minutes in a steamer (or a large stockpot set up as a steamer). Check if the fish is done by piercing it with a sharp knife. The flesh should be fully opaque and should come off the bone easily. The exact cooking time may vary depending on the size of your fish.

5. Serve the fish wrapped, with lime or lemon wedges on the side.

Goan Fish Curry

Serves 2 as a main

*****

1½ tbsp coconut oil,
   or any neutral oil

10–12 curry leaves

75g onions, thinly sliced

1 tsp garlic paste

½ tsp ground turmeric

300ml coconut milk

4–6 pieces of dried kokum,
   or 1½ tbsp tamarind paste

2 green chillies, slit lengthways

1 tsp sugar, or to taste

1 tsp salt, or to taste

800g sea bream, cut into steaks
   4cm thick, or sea bream, sea
   bass, halibut or turbot fillets

lime wedges and red onion rings,
   to serve

*****

For the masala

1 tsp cumin seeds

1½ tbsp coriander seeds

½ tsp black peppercorns

8 Kashmiri red chillies, stems and
   seeds removed

When I was growing up, every summer holiday my parents, brother and I would head to Goa. We stayed at the same resort each year, and even as a nine-year-old I would find my way into the kitchen to befriend the chefs and the restaurant team. The executive chef, Urbano Rego, was one of my greatest culinary influences, and I remember eating some of our most memorable meals cooked by him. His fish curry was exquisite, and always the first thing we'd eat upon arriving in Goa, served simply with brown Goan rice and a salad of cucumbers, tomatoes, carrots and onions. This recipe is the closest I have come to recreating Chef Rego's magic in my own kitchen.

1. Heat a small dry pan over a medium heat and toast the cumin seeds, coriander seeds and black peppercorns for the masala for about 2 minutes until fragrant.

2. Put the toasted spices and Kashmiri red chillies into a bowl. Add a little warm water to soak the chillies until they soften, ideally overnight. Then blend to a fine paste, adding more water if required. Set aside.

3. Heat the coconut oil in a large pan over a medium heat. Add the curry leaves and sliced onions and cook for about 4–5 minutes until the onions soften and go translucent.

4. Add the garlic paste and cook for another minute, then stir in the turmeric and the masala paste. Cook for about 5 minutes over a low heat until the oil begins to separate from the masala and comes to the surface.

5. Pour in the coconut milk along with 200ml of water, mixing well to combine, then bring to a gentle simmer. Add the kokum (or tamarind paste), green chillies, sugar and salt, and continue cooking for 6–8 minutes.

6. Add the fish steaks or fillets to the pan, cover and simmer for about 20 minutes, or until the sauce has reduced to the consistency of double cream. To prevent the fish breaking up, avoid stirring; instead, gently shake the pan.

7. Check the seasoning, adding more salt or sugar to balance the flavours. Serve hot, with a wedge of lime and some red onion rings.

Baked Mustard Fish

Serves 2 as a main

*****

1 tsp ground turmeric

500–700g hilsa, mackerel, bream, salmon or trout, cut into steaks or fillets (see notes, right)

1 tbsp black mustard seeds

2 tbsp yellow mustard seeds

2 tbsp white poppy seeds

1 garlic clove, grated

1cm ginger, grated

150–200g Greek-style yoghurt

½ tsp sugar

1 tbsp mustard oil

1 tsp nigella seeds

2 green chillies, slit in half lengthwise (optional)

salt, to taste

I grew up eating this at a Bengali friend's home in Mumbai, and it's right up there among my top ten Indian dishes, especially when cooked with hilsa (ilish), an oily fish celebrated with fervour in East India and Bangladesh. The mere mention of hilsa sparks excitement in the hearts of many Bengalis. The fish has a distinctively sweet flavour and is usually available in the frozen section at Bangladeshi or large Indian grocers. I encourage you to try this recipe if you ever come across the fish. Remember, though, that while delicious, it's an incredibly bony fish and makes you work hard for your reward! You can substitute it with any oily fish like mackerel, shad or herring, or you can even make this dish with salmon, trout or bream.

All you need on the side is some plain rice or some Mustard Mashed Potatoes (pictured; see page 165) and, if you're feeling indulgent, a few pieces of Spicy Fried Aubergine (see page 166).

1. Mix 2 tablespoons of water with ½ teaspoon of turmeric and ½ teaspoon of salt in a bowl, and marinate the fish in this for 15–20 minutes at room temperature while you prepare the rest of the ingredients.

2. Combine the rest of the turmeric, both mustard seeds and the poppy seeds in the jar of a spice grinder and grind them to a fine powder. Be careful not to add any liquid or they won't grind as finely. Once ground, add the garlic, ginger and a couple of tablespoons of the yoghurt and continue grinding to a beautiful smooth, mustardy paste.

3. Mix the paste with the remaining yoghurt and the sugar and season to taste.

4. Preheat the oven to 180°C fan.

5. Place the marinated fish in a small ovenproof dish, pour the paste over and mix well. Sprinkle over the mustard oil, nigella seeds and slit chillies, then cover tightly with foil and bake for 20 minutes, or longer, depending on the size of your fish.

6. Serve hot.

MEAT
and
POULTRY

Reshmi Chicken Tikka

**Serves 4 as a main or
8 as a snack or starter**

*****

1kg chicken legs, skinless and
  boneless, cut into 5cm pieces
metal or wooden skewers
  (if using wooden skewers,
  soak in water for 30 minutes to
  prevent burning)
melted butter, for basting
  and serving
1 tsp chaat masala (see page 266
  for homemade)
1 tbsp chopped fresh coriander
lime wedges and sliced red onion
  rings, to garnish

*****

For the first marinade

1 tsp ginger paste
1 tbsp garlic paste
1 tsp salt
juice of 1 lime

*****

For the second marinade

1 tsp ginger paste
1 tsp garlic paste
1 tsp kasoori methi (dried
  fenugreek leaves)
1 tsp ground white pepper
1 tbsp garam masala
200g Greek-style yoghurt
200ml double cream
2 tbsp grated Cheddar cheese
6 green cardamom pods, seeds
  crushed to a powder
2 tbsp melted butter
1 tsp salt

Growing up in Mumbai, sports clubs were the epicentres of social life. The caterers at these clubs were often just as renowned as the sporting facilities they offered. The Cricket Club of India, fondly known as CCI, where the iconic Brabourne Stadium is located, was my favourite. We spent countless evenings and weekends there, swimming, playing sports and socializing with friends and family. Every evening, cane chairs and tables would be arranged on the lawns, and the chefs would light up charcoal barbecues to serve freshly grilled kebabs, tikkas and chaats. Sitting there, enjoying these treats while watching the sun dip into the Arabian Sea, is one of my most vivid food memories from Mumbai.

My go-to dish was always the reshmi chicken tikka, a chicken skewer marinated in spiced yoghurt and cooked in the tandoor – usually enjoyed as a roll wrapped in a paper-thin rumali roti along with fresh mint chutney and a salad of finely sliced carrots and onions. You can recreate this at home with Fulkas (page 208), Lachcha Onions (page 179) and Green Chutney (page 196).

1. Mix all the ingredients for the first marinade in a large mixing bowl and coat the chicken pieces in it. Cover the chicken and refrigerate for 30 minutes.

2. After 30 minutes, mix all the ingredients for the second marinade. Rub it all over the chicken, cover, and let it rest in the fridge for 2–3 hours, or better still, overnight.

3. Thread the chicken onto skewers and cook over a hot barbecue. Alternatively, bake in the oven at 200–220°C fan for 8–10 minutes.

4. Crank up the temperature of the barbecue (or oven) to maximum, baste the chicken with melted butter, and cook for another 4–6 minutes until charred in spots and fully cooked through.

5. Drizzle with a little more melted butter and sprinkle with chaat masala and chopped coriander before serving, with lime wedges and red onion rings on the side.

Proper Butter Chicken

Serves 4 as a main or

6–8 as a starter or snack

*****

1kg chicken legs, skinless, on
the bone, cut into thighs and
drumsticks

red onion rings, to garnish

*****

For the first marinade

1 tsp ground turmeric

1 tsp Kashmiri red chilli powder

1 tsp salt

juice of ½ lime

*****

For the second marinade

1 tbsp ginger paste

1 tbsp garlic paste

1 tsp kasoori methi (dried
fenugreek leaves)

1 tsp ground white pepper

1 tbsp garam masala (see page
267 for homemade)

1 tbsp red chilli paste (see
page 15), or 1 tsp Kashmiri
red chilli powder

100g Greek-style yoghurt

2 tbsp melted butter, plus more
to baste

1 tsp salt

*****

For the finishing sauce

150ml single cream,
at room temperature

30–50g melted butter

1 tsp chaat masala (see page 266
for homemade)

1 tbsp finely chopped fresh
coriander

a pinch of kasoori methi (optional)

a pinch of salt (optional)

When you think of butter chicken, you probably envisage a glorious, silky tomato sauce laden with cream and butter, balanced with sweetness, delicate spices and succulent chicken morsels. My image of this dish was no different, until a friend took me to a streetside stall in Old Delhi. Famous for their unique spin on butter chicken, this version had no tomatoes – just perfectly charred chicken, a generous splash of cream, and loads of butter. I never got the recipe from them, but after years of trial and error, I managed to reverse-engineer my own version. This has been an easy-to-make showstopper at many barbecues since then and all it needs on the side are some fresh, pillowy Naans (page 224) and Lachcha Onions (page 179). You can try the recipe with wings or boneless thighs too, adjusting the cooking time as required.

For the more traditional tomato-based curry, check out the Chicken Makhani on page 144.

1. Score the chicken thighs and legs to allow the marinade to penetrate and the meat to cook more quickly. Sprinkle over the turmeric, chilli powder, salt and lime juice and mix well. This simple first marinade is a primary layer of flavour, before the second richer marinade goes on. Cover the chicken and refrigerate for 30 minutes.

2. After 30 minutes, mix all the ingredients for the second marinade. Rub it all over the chicken, cover and let it rest in the fridge for 2–3 hours, or better still, overnight.

3. Cook the chicken over a hot barbecue (or bake in the oven at 140–160°C fan) for 25 minutes to ensure it cooks through.

4. Crank up the temperature of the barbecue (or oven) to maximum. Baste the chicken with some more melted butter and cook for another 8–10 minutes until slightly charred and wonderfully smoky.

5. In a mixing bowl, combine the ingredients for the finishing sauce: cream, butter, chaat masala, fresh coriander and kasoori methi (if using). Add the cooked chicken, mix thoroughly and check the seasoning, adding a pinch of salt if required.

6. Garnish with red onion rings and serve immediately.

Seekh Kebabs

**Serves 6 as a starter
or snack**

*****

1kg lamb mince, at least 20% fat

metal or wooden skewers
(if using wooden skewers,
soak in water for 30 minutes to
prevent burning)

melted butter or oil, for basting
and serving

1 tsp chaat masala (see page 266
for homemade)

2 tbsp chopped fresh coriander,
to garnish

*****

For the marinade

2 tsp coriander seeds

1 tsp cumin seeds

1 tsp fennel seeds

1 tsp Kashmiri red chilli powder

½ tsp ground turmeric

2 tsp garam masala (see page 267
for homemade)

½ tsp finely ground black pepper

2 tbsp finely chopped fresh mint
leaves

2 tbsp finely chopped fresh
coriander leaves

2 green chillies, finely chopped

3 tsp finely grated Cheddar
cheese

3 garlic cloves, grated

2.5cm ginger, grated

1 egg

juice of ½ a lime

1 tsp salt, to taste

These spiced minced meat skewers have their roots in Persian cuisine, and while you can find variations of spiced lamb, beef and chicken skewers across south Asia and the Middle East, the seekh kebabs commonly enjoyed in India and Pakistan are my favourite. They are richly seasoned with a blend of fresh herbs, spices, ginger and garlic, then cooked in a tandoor until they develop a beautiful char on the outside while staying moist and juicy on the inside. I add eggs and cheese to help bind the mixture and add extra flavour.

To ensure your kebabs turn out perfectly, use a fatty mince to prevent them drying out and only apply a thin layer of meat to the skewers, so that the exterior doesn't overcook while the inside remains underdone. My preferred cooking method is to cook them over charcoal. The sweet smoke infuses the kebabs as the fat drips down on to the smouldering coals, taking them to the next level.

1. Start by toasting the coriander, cumin and fennel seeds in a dry pan over a medium heat for a minute until fragrant. Set them aside in a bowl until fully cooled, then grind to a fine powder.

2. Mix the freshly ground spice powder with the remaining marinade ingredients. Once fully combined, add the lamb and mix thoroughly. Cover the mixture and let it rest in the fridge for an hour or two.

3. Take a small portion (about half a handful) of the meat mixture and shape it around a skewer, pressing it tightly to form a long, cylindrical kebab. Ensure that the kebab is evenly shaped and firmly attached to the skewer. To make this easier, wet your hands in a bowl filled with water before handling the meat to prevent it sticking to your hands.

4. *If cooking in the oven:* Preheat the grill to high and place a foil-lined tray lined on the middle shelf. Once the tray is hot, place the skewers on it. Grill for 8–10 minutes, turning halfway and basting with melted butter. If the skewers haven't begun browning after 8 minutes, brush them with butter, move the tray to the top shelf and continue to cook directly under the grill for 2–3 minutes, turning the skewers every minute.

If cooking on the stove: Heat a heavy pan over a medium-high heat. Melt a teaspoon of butter and when it starts to brown, add the skewers and cook for 8–10 minutes, turning to ensure they colour evenly on all sides.

If cooking on the barbecue: Place the skewers on a well-oiled rack directly over the flames and cook for 6–8 minutes, turning every couple of minutes. Make sure the rack is very hot before placing the skewers on it, to avoid them sticking. The exact cooking time will depend on the height of the rack and the temperature.

5. Drizzle the skewers with melted butter and sprinkle over the chaat masala and fresh coriander before serving.

Home-style Chicken Curry

Serves 4 as a main

*****

2 tbsp ghee

1 tsp cumin seeds

5cm cassia bark or cinnamon stick

3 black cardamom pods

4 green cardamom pods

4 cloves

1 tsp black peppercorns

2 bay leaves

250g red onions, thinly sliced

2 tsp salt, or to taste

1 tbsp ginger paste

1 tbsp garlic paste

1kg chicken legs, skinless, on the
   bone, cut into 5cm pieces

¾ tbsp Kashmiri chilli powder

1 tbsp ground cumin

2 tbsp ground coriander

¾ tsp ground turmeric

200g ripe tomatoes, finely
   chopped (or 150g tinned
   chopped tomatoes)

2 green chillies, slit lengthways

fresh coriander, finely chopped,
   to garnish

Almost every meat-eating family in north India has their own take on this quick and easy chicken curry. I cooked this recipe weekly when I lived in Delhi, where it enjoys the same cherished place in Punjabi homes as chicken tikka masala does in British Indian restaurants. Lighter and fresher than butter chicken or tikka masala, it is perfect served alongside a simple vegetable dish, some dal and freshly made Fulkas (page 208) or plain rice.

   When cooking Indian curries I always use skinless chicken legs or thighs on the bone. Chicken breast tends to dry out, and boneless chicken just doesn't give the dish the same depth of flavour. Since Indian cuisine rarely uses stocks, cooking with bone-in meat creates a rich, flavourful broth as the dish simmers.

1. Warm the ghee in a heavy pan set over a medium heat.

2. Add the cumin seeds, cassia bark, both types of cardamom, the cloves, peppercorns and bay leaves and cook for a minute, until aromatic.

3. Add the onions with ½ teaspoon of salt to help them cook evenly. Once they turn translucent and become soft, about 5 minutes, add the ginger and garlic pastes and cook for 2–3 minutes until everything is lightly brown, adding a splash of water if required.

4. Add the chicken, then raise the temperature to medium-high and cook, stirring constantly, until light brown, about 4–5 minutes. Add the ground spices and cook for 2 minutes.

5. Add the tomatoes along with 250–300ml of water and 1½ teaspoons of salt, then cover and simmer over a low heat until the chicken is fully cooked, 12–15 minutes. Add the slit green chillies for the final 3 minutes.

6. Check that you are happy with the seasoning and garnish with fresh coriander before serving. This curry, like many others, can be made up to a couple of days in advance and will only taste better when reheated after a night or two in the fridge.

Chettinad Chicken Curry

Serves 4 as a main

*****

1kg chicken thighs, skinless, on
  the bone, cut into 5cm pieces

¼ tsp ground turmeric

1 tsp ginger paste

1 tsp garlic paste

½ tsp each of salt and pepper

*****

For the Chettinad masala

3 dried red chillies, stems and
  seeds removed

4 green cardamom pods

3–4 pieces of black stone flower
  (see right)

1 tsp black peppercorns

1 tsp fennel seeds

½ tsp cumin seeds

1 tbsp coriander seeds

1 cinnamon stick

4 cloves

1 bay leaf (optional)

3 tbsp desiccated coconut

*****

For the curry

2 tbsp coconut oil

1 medium red onion

2 tsp salt, or to taste

2 tsp ginger paste

2 tsp garlic paste

10–12 curry leaves

350g ripe fresh tomatoes, finely
  chopped (or 200g tinned
  chopped tomatoes)

green chillies, slit in half
  lengthways, to garnish

red onion rings, to garnish

This is one of my favourite chicken curries from the Chettinad region of south India. I know it's pretty ingredient-heavy, but don't let that put you off. Most of the spices can be bought from specialist South Asian grocers, or online, and can be used in a number of other Indian recipes.

  The defining spice in this curry is the black stone flower (it's also known as kalpasi or patthar phool if you're searching for it in a shop), a dried lichen with an earthy flavour. When you make this curry, I suggest making a big batch of the Chettinad masala – it will store well for months and I'm confident, once you've eaten it once, you'll be making this curry again and again.

1. Mix together the chicken, turmeric, ginger and garlic pastes, and salt and pepper. Let it marinate for 30 minutes, or better still, overnight in the fridge.

2. To make the Chettinad masala, toast all the spices in a dry pan over a medium heat for 3–4 minutes, until they darken slightly and become aromatic. Transfer them to a large bowl or plate to cool. In the same pan, roast the coconut until it turns golden and aromatic, being careful not to burn it. Once cooled, mix the coconut with the toasted spices and grind everything to a fine powder, using a spice grinder or a small blender. Grinding the powder finely ensures a smooth curry texture.

3. For the curry, heat the coconut oil in a heavy pan over a medium heat. Add the onion with ½ teaspoon of salt and cook for 4–5 minutes, until light brown. (To save time, you can use 80g of fried brown onions along with a splash of water – see page 12.)

4. Add the ginger and garlic pastes, cook for another 2 minutes, then add the curry leaves and the marinated chicken. Increase the temperature to high and cook until the chicken caramelizes, about 5–6 minutes. Reduce the heat to medium and add the Chettinad masala. Cook for a minute, then add the tomatoes and 1½ teaspoons of salt. Continue cooking until the curry thickens and darkens, about 12–15 minutes, adding a splash of water every now and then if the spices begin to stick to the pan. I prefer this curry quite dry, but you can add some water or coconut milk if you want gravy. Check the seasoning before taking it off the heat.

5. Serve garnished with slit green chillies and red onion rings.

Achari Chicken, Two Ways

Achar translates as 'pickle' in Hindi, and achari chicken is cooked with spices typically used in north Indian pickles – fenugreek, nigella, mustard and fennel seeds are all tempered in pungent mustard oil. It's a dish that tests your spice collection. If you're short on some or not keen on expanding your larder, use the store-bought pickle hack below.

I've provided two equally effective, yet very different, ways to cook this unique dish. The traditional method uses a pan, wok or kadhai, resulting in a delicious meat curry, while the easier traybake version produces a fantastic single-tray weeknight meal or a centrepiece for an alternative Sunday roast.

While I recommend making the achari spice mix from scratch (see recipe on page 140), for a quicker version you can use 2 tablespoons of store-bought spicy mango or green chilli pickle. Be sure to find the most authentic Punjabi pickle you can, and avoid using sweet pickles or mango chutney. If you're using a Punjabi pickle, these are usually made with mustard oil, so you can swap the mustard oil in the recipe for any neutral oil unless you already have mustard oil to hand.

Achari Traybake

Serves 4 as a main

*****

1.5kg chicken legs, skinless, cut
   into thighs and drumsticks

250ml chicken stock

1 tbsp tomato purée

1 head of garlic, cut in half through
   the middle

5cm ginger, sliced in half
   horizontally

1 large red onion, cut into 6 cubes

a handful of Padrón peppers
   (optional)

a pinch of salt

1 tbsp mustard oil

1 tbsp apple cider vinegar

*****

For the marinade

1½ tsp Kashmiri red chilli powder

½ tsp ground turmeric

1 tsp garlic paste

2 tsp ginger paste

2 tbsp mustard oil
   (or any neutral oil)

250g Greek-style yoghurt

3 tbsp Punjabi chilli pickle or
   mango pickle

1½ tsp salt

*****

To garnish

juice of ½ lime

5cm ginger, cut into matchsticks

1 small red onion, cut into
   thin rings

1 tbsp chopped fresh coriander

This is a great centrepiece for an alternative Sunday roast. I like to use a whole spatchcocked chicken weighing 1.2–1.5kg for this. Follow the same recipe, adding about 10 minutes to the cooking time in step 5 below. If, on the other hand, you are cooking for one, simply quarter this recipe and cook it in an air fryer at 180°C for 25–30 minutes.

For a vegetarian achari traybake, try this recipe with a whole cauliflower and substitute the chicken stock with vegetable stock. Marinate the cauliflower in step 1 for about 10 minutes, then wrap it and roast it alongside the vegetables in step 4. Unwrap, drizzle with some oil or melted butter, place on top of the vegetables and roast for about 15–20 minutes in step 5. Finally place under the grill for 3–4 minutes on max heat to colour, if it hasn't already browned evenly.

1. Mix the ingredients for the marinade and rub all over the chicken pieces. Refrigerate the marinated chicken for at least 2 hours, or ideally overnight. The salt, ginger and garlic ensure that the meat stays succulent and moist, so don't skip this step! Mix any leftover marinade with the stock and tomato purée, and set aside. We will add this yoghurty stock to the roasting tray later to create the tastiest sauce.

2. Take the chicken out of the fridge 30 minutes before cooking – this ensures it doesn't overcook on the outside while staying raw on the inside. Preheat the oven to 200°C fan.

3. When ready to cook, toss the garlic, ginger, onion and peppers (if using) in salt and oil and place in a tray or wide dish that's large enough to accommodate the chicken on top later. Roast the vegetables in the oven for about 8 minutes, until just beginning to colour.

4. Add the yoghurt, stock mixture and the vinegar to the oven tray and mix it into the vegetables using a spoon. Place the chicken pieces on top of the vegetables and roast for 30–40 minutes, giving the tray a little shake and stir halfway through.

5. If at any point the chicken starts to colour too much, cover loosely with a piece of foil. Conversely, if the bird doesn't colour, raise the temperature to 220°C fan for the final 15 minutes.

6. Once fully cooked, squeeze over the lime juice and garnish with ginger, onion rings and coriander.

Achari Curry

Serves 4 as a main

*****

1kg chicken, thighs or legs, skin
    removed, on the bone

*****

For the marinade

2 tsp Kashmiri red chilli powder

1 tsp ground turmeric

1 tsp ginger paste

1 tsp garlic paste

250g Greek-style yoghurt

2 green chillies, finely chopped

1 tbsp mustard oil

1 tsp salt

*****

For the achari spice mix

1 tsp black (or yellow) mustard
    seeds

2 tsp fennel seeds

2 tsp coriander seeds

1 tsp cumin seeds

1 tsp fenugreek seeds

*****

For the curry

1 tbsp mustard oil

1 tsp cumin seeds

1 tsp nigella seeds

1 tbsp ginger paste

1 tbsp garlic paste

2 ripe tomatoes, chopped

1 tsp kasoori methi (dried
    fenugreek leaves)

2 tbsp apple cider vinegar (or juice
    of ½ lime)

*****

To garnish

1 small red onion, cut into rings

1 tbsp chopped fresh coriander

5cm ginger, cut into matchsticks

This traditional north Indian curry features classic Indian pickling (achari) spices. While I recommend making the achari spice mix from scratch, see page 136 for a quick hack using store-bought pickle instead.

For a vegetarian alternative, paneer is a great substitute for chicken. If using raw paneer, reduce the cooking time in step 5 to 2 minutes, or skip it completely if using fried paneer.

1. Mix the chicken with all the ingredients for the marinade and set aside for anywhere between 30 minutes to overnight in the fridge.

2. Toast the ingredients for the achari spice mix in a dry pan set over a low heat, stirring constantly, until fragrant and the seeds are just beginning to change colour. This can take 3–5 minutes, and I would suggest erring on the side of caution and taking them off early if in doubt. If they burn, there's no recovery! Once the seeds cool, grind them to a coarse powder in a pestle and mortar or spice grinder.

3. Heat the oil in a wok, kadhai or wide pan over a medium heat.

4. Add the cumin and nigella seeds and when they begin to crackle, add the ginger and garlic pastes and cook for 2 minutes until aromatic, being careful not to brown the pastes.

5. Now add the chicken and cook it over a medium-high heat until lightly browned, about 2–3 minutes. You may need to add a splash of water from time to time to prevent the ginger and garlic sticking to the pan.

6. Once the chicken has browned, add the achari spice mix and the tomatoes and cook for 5–7 minutes, until the tomatoes have broken down into a thick paste and coat the chicken.

7. Add any remaining marinade and 150–200ml of water, along with the kasoori methi and vinegar, then cover the pan and cook for a further 6–8 minutes. I like the curry fairly thick, but you can add more water if you prefer more gravy.

8. Season with salt to your taste and garnish with onion rings, coriander and ginger before serving.

Badami Chicken

Serves 4 as a main

*****

1kg chicken thighs, skinless, on
    the bone, cut into 5cm pieces

2 tbsp ghee

250g onions, thinly sliced

1 tsp salt, or to taste

200g Greek-style yoghurt

100ml single cream

2 green chillies, slit lengthways

1 tsp kasoori methi (dried
    fenugreek leaves)

½ tsp garam masala (see
    page 267 for homemade)

1 medium red onion, cut into rings,
    to garnish

*****

For the marinade

1 tbsp ginger paste

1 tbsp garlic paste

½ tsp Kashmiri red chilli powder

½ tsp ground turmeric

½ tsp salt

*****

For the masala

3 green cardamom pods

3–4 cloves

1 tsp black peppercorns

1 dried red chilli, stem and
    seeds removed

100g almonds, toasted

Mughlai cuisine originated in the royal kitchens of the Mughal emperors, known for their complex and indulgent dishes crafted by skilled chefs and made with expensive spices. Over time, these spices have become more accessible, and the term 'Mughlai cuisine' now tends to represent the richer dishes typically found in north Indian restaurants across India. These dishes are not usually cooked at home, due to the time and special equipment they require. This recipe is a simplified version of a distinctive Mughlai-style chicken dish, cooked in a glorious yoghurt gravy thickened with ground almonds and caramelized onions. It makes a stunning centrepiece for a dinner party, served with Black Dal (page 72), Fulkas (page 208) or Parathas (page 216), and Lachcha Onions (page 179).

1. Mix together all the ingredients for the marinade in a bowl and coat the chicken in it. Cover and refrigerate for 2 hours, or ideally overnight.

2. To make the masala, toast the cardamom pods, cloves, peppercorns and chilli in a dry pan over a medium heat for 2 minutes until the spices are aromatic. Once cooled, mix with the toasted almonds and grind everything to a fine powder using a spice grinder or a small blender. Avoid leaving the grinder running for too long or the oil from the almonds will split, turning it to butter; keep pulsing the mixer or blender instead. Grind the mixture as finely as possible for a smooth-textured curry.

3. Heat the ghee in a heavy pan over a medium heat. Add the onions and ½ teaspoon of salt and cook for 10–12 minutes until deep brown. (To save time, use 120g of fried brown onions with a splash of water – see page 12.)

4. Add the marinated chicken and cook for 4–5 minutes over a high heat to brown it. Reduce the heat, add the masala and cook for another 2 minutes.

5. Take the pan off the heat and add the yoghurt and cream, stirring continuously to prevent the sauce splitting, then return to the heat and cook for a minute. Add the chillies, kasoori methi and garam masala, then pour in 100ml of water, cover and cook for 15–20 minutes.

6. Add ½ teaspoon of salt, and cook uncovered until the curry reaches your desired consistency. Check the seasoning before serving. I prefer a semi-dry curry with a thick gravy, but you can add some water if you prefer a thinner consistency. Garnish with onion rings to serve.

Chicken Makhani

Serves 4 as a main

*****

800g skinless, boneless chicken
thighs, cut into 5cm pieces

*****

For the marinade

150g Greek-style yoghurt

1 tsp ground turmeric

2 tsp Kashmiri red chilli powder

½ tsp salt

1 tsp garam masala (see page 267
for homemade)

1 tbsp lime juice

1 tsp garlic paste

1 tsp ginger paste

2 tbsp melted butter

*****

For the curry

3 tbsp vegetable oil

200g onions, finely chopped

1 tsp salt, or to taste

1 tsp garlic paste

1 tsp ginger paste

800g fresh ripe tomatoes,
finely chopped (or 650g
tinned tomatoes)

1 tbsp tomato purée

1 tsp ground coriander

1 tsp garam masala (see page 267
for homemade)

1 tsp kasoori methi (dried
fenugreek leaves)

1 tbsp Kashmiri red chilli powder

200ml double cream, plus a few
more tablespoons to garnish

1 tbsp honey

Arguably one of the most famous Indian dishes, this iconic chicken curry goes by many names – chicken tikka masala, butter chicken, chicken makhanwala, and more. At its core, a great chicken makhani (literally meaning buttery chicken) begins with barbecued or grilled chicken that is succulent, flavourful and beautifully charred. The smokiness from the chicken infuses the silky tomato and cream gravy, which is delicately spiced with cardamom and dried fenugreek leaves. Serve with flatbreads.

The vibrant red colour frequently associated with this dish sadly comes from artificial food colouring. To achieve a natural, bright hue, I recommend using the highest quality Kashmiri red chilli powder you can find. This chilli powder is milder than most, adding a wonderful colour and flavour to the dish without overwhelming heat.

1. Mix all the ingredients for the marinade in a large bowl. Add the chicken, coat well, then cover and refrigerate for 2 hours, or ideally overnight.

2. Once marinated, barbecue, bake or air-fry the chicken on maximum heat for 10–15 minutes, until charred in spots. Don't worry if the chicken hasn't cooked through fully, it will be simmered in the curry later. The purpose of this step is to char the chicken, giving the curry a smoky flavour.

3. Heat the oil in a large pan over a medium heat and add the chopped onions, along with a pinch of salt to help them cook evenly. Cook until they start to brown slightly, about 5–6 minutes, then add the garlic and ginger pastes and cook for another 2 minutes until fragrant. Stir in the chopped tomatoes and tomato purée, cooking until the mixture thickens and the oil starts to separate from the sauce, about 10–12 minutes.

4. Add the coriander, garam masala, kasoori methi and chilli powder to the tomato mixture and cook for 2 minutes. Lower the heat and stir in the cream, honey and ¾ teaspoon of salt, mixing to create a smooth sauce. Simmer for 10 minutes, adding about 100ml of water if it gets too thick.

5. Add the cooked chicken to the pan, along with any cooking juices and 1 teaspoon of salt. Stir to coat the chicken in the sauce, then simmer for an additional 10–12 minutes to make sure it is cooked through. Check the seasoning and add more salt or honey to your taste.

6. Garnish with an extra dollop of cream and serve.

Kheema Matar

Serves 4 as a main

*****

3 tbsp neutral oil or ghee

1 tsp cumin seeds

2 bay leaves

4 cloves

5cm piece of cassia bark or
   cinnamon stick

1 star anise (optional)

1 tsp black peppercorns

250g onions, finely chopped

1 tbsp garlic paste

1 tbsp ginger paste

2 green chillies, finely chopped

1kg minced lamb or beef

3 tbsp Greek-style yoghurt
   (optional)

½ tsp ground turmeric

1 tbsp Kashmiri red chilli powder

1 tsp ground cumin

1 tbsp ground coriander

400g fresh ripe tomatoes, finely
   chopped (or 300g tinned
   chopped tomatoes)

200g peas (fresh or frozen)

1 tbsp kasoori methi (dried
   fenugreek leaves)

1½ tsp salt, to taste

1 tsp garam masala (see page 267
   for homemade)

2 tbsp finely chopped fresh
   coriander leaves, plus extra
   to garnish

1 small onion, finely chopped,
   to garnish

1 lime or lemon, cut into wedges,
   to serve

This mince and pea dish is a favourite in most meat-eating homes in the north. I love how the sweetness of the green peas complements the rich, buttery, spiced lamb mince. Though it may seem simple, there are a few crucial steps to ensure you achieve that perfect, melt-in-the-mouth texture of a great kheema matar. First, make sure you're using medium-fat mince. I prefer to have the butcher mince the meat in front of me so I can see exactly what's going into it, choosing a mix of shoulder and neck cuts, passed through the mincer twice for a finer texture. While lamb or goat mince is ideal for this dish, beef can be a good substitute as well.

Another crucial step is properly browning the meat. Cook the meat in batches to avoid overcrowding the pan, which can cause the meat to boil instead of fry. Listen and look out for that wonderful sizzle. Browning meat adds depth of flavour and helps it break down later in the cooking process, preventing a gritty, chewy texture in the final dish.

Serve with plain rice or flatbreads (I like to stuff it in burger buns, too).

1. Heat the oil or ghee in a large pan over a medium heat. Add the cumin seeds, bay leaves, cloves, cassia bark, star anise and peppercorns. Fry for a minute until the spices are fragrant. Add the finely chopped onions and cook until they turn golden brown, about 8–10 minutes. (To save time, use 3 tablespoons of fried brown onions with a splash of water – see page 12.) Add the garlic and ginger pastes and green chillies and cook for a minute.

2. Turn the heat up to high and add the minced meat to the pan, breaking it up with a spoon. Cook until the meat is evenly browned, 6–8 minutes. You may need to cook the meat in batches. If the meat releases too much moisture, let it evaporate before continuing.

3. Stir in the yoghurt, turmeric, chilli powder, cumin and ground coriander. Cook for a minute, then add the tomatoes and mix well. Add 200ml of water, cover and cook for 25–30 minutes over a medium heat, stirring frequently. Once most of the liquid has evaporated and the meat is tender, take the lid off and keep cooking until you reach your desired consistency.

4. Add the peas and mix well, then add the kasoori methi, salt and garam masala and cook for another 5–6 minutes, until the peas are tender. Stir in the coriander and cook for a final minute.

5. Garnish with chopped onion, extra coriander and lime or lemon wedges.

BBQ Lamb Chop Curry

Serves 4 as a main

*****

8 lamb chops

2 tbsp chopped fresh coriander
  leaves, to garnish

½ a red onion, finely sliced,
  to garnish

*****

For the marinade

½ tsp ginger paste

½ tsp garlic paste

¼ tsp ground turmeric

1 tsp Kashmiri red chilli powder

1 tbsp Greek-style yoghurt

1 tbsp ghee

½ tsp sea salt

*****

For the curry

1 onion

2 large tomatoes

2 tbsp ghee

3 cloves

3 green cardamom pods

8cm cinnamon stick

1 bay leaf

½ tbsp ginger paste

½ tbsp garlic paste

½ tsp ground turmeric

½ tsp ground cumin

½ tsp ground coriander

1 tsp garam masala (see page 267
  for homemade)

½ tsp Kashmiri red chilli powder

a pinch of salt

1 tbsp tomato purée

People are crazy for mutton chop curries in the Indian subcontinent. Many north Indian and Pakistani recipes call for chops to be simmered in gravy for hours, drawing out deep flavours from the bones and tenderizing the meat. In the West, however, these recipes are often taken at face value and cooks use tender lamb chops instead. This is a fundamental mistake. In India, what we refer to as mutton chops are actually goat. These are much tougher than the tender lamb chops or cutlets typically found in Western butchers and supermarkets. Lamb chops are lean and are best served medium or medium rare – a texture that's lost after hours of slow simmering in a curry. Not to mention that lamb chops are pricey and slow cooking them to dry in a curry is hardly the best use of your money. Goat chops take longer to cook and are best stewed, so they work perfectly well.

   With this in mind, I crafted my ideal lamb chop curry for a barbecue. This recipe is a nod to traditional curries but incorporates my love of live fire cooking, combining layers of flavour with perfectly cooked, smoky chops. Serve with Fulkas (page 208), Naans (page 224) or plain rice.

1. Combine the marinade ingredients in a mixing bowl, add the chops and coat well. Leave to rest for 30 minutes, or ideally overnight in the fridge.

2. When your barbecue is ready, place the onion directly on the coals or over the fire. Cook for 5–10 minutes, until it's fully charred on the outside but soft inside. In the last minute, add the tomatoes to the fire to let them char and soften as well. Once done, allow the vegetables to cool, then peel and chop them as finely as possible and set aside. If you're cooking indoors, char the vegetables on a gas hob or under a hot grill. Cooking times will vary depending on your heat source and temperature.

3. Heat the ghee in a heavy pan over a medium heat. Add the cloves, cardamom pods, cinnamon and bay leaf, and cook for a minute, then add the ginger and garlic pastes and cook for 2–3 minutes. Add the ground spices and salt and cook for 30 seconds, adding a splash of water if needed. Stir in the tomato purée, chopped tomatoes and onion, along with 200ml of water, and cook over a low heat for about 8–10 minutes until you have a rich, velvety curry.

4. In the meantime, grill the marinated chops directly over the heat until they are nicely charred, about 2–3 minutes on each side. Transfer the chops to the curry and let them simmer for another 3–5 minutes over a low heat.

5. Garnish with fresh coriander and sliced onions and serve.

Parsi Sali Boti

Serves 4–6 as a main

*****

1.5kg lamb, mutton or goat
   shoulder or neck, on the bone,
   cut into 2.5–5cm cubes

1 tbsp finely chopped fresh
   coriander leaves, to garnish

50g potato straws (sali) or salted
   potato crisps, to garnish

*****

For the marinade

1 tsp ground turmeric

1 tbsp ginger paste

1 tbsp garlic paste

½ tsp salt

*****

For the curry

3 tbsp neutral oil or ghee

2 bay leaves

5cm cassia bark or cinnamon stick

4 cloves

4 green cardamom pods

250g onions, finely chopped

1½ tsp salt, or to taste

1 tbsp ginger paste

1 tbsp garlic paste

1 tbsp Kashmiri red chilli powder

1 tsp ground cumin

1 tbsp ground coriander

1 tsp garam masala (see page 267
   for homemade)

500g fresh ripe tomatoes, finely
   chopped (or 400g tinned
   chopped tomatoes)

2 green chillies, slit lengthways

1 tbsp jaggery or sugar, to taste

2–3 tbsp malt vinegar, or white
   wine vinegar

I grew up with a number of close Parsi friends at school and university in Mumbai and we'd often eat this dish at their homes. A tender meat curry topped with crispy potato straws, it was an instant hit with diners of all ages. While you can find potato straws labelled as 'sali' or 'salli' at Indian grocers, and 'potato sticks' or 'potato straws' at large Western supermarkets, I sometimes crumble a bag of crisps over the curry at home for a similarly satisfying crunch.

   This dish is equally delicious when made with chicken. Use skinless thighs or legs, keeping them on the bone, and adjust the water and cooking time accordingly. I occasionally add dried apricots to the dish for a sweet, fruity adaptation of this dish called jardalu sali boti. I love eating this with Fulkas (page 208), pav, bread rolls or sliced white bread.

1. Mix together all the ingredients for the marinade in a bowl and rub them into the meat, then allow it to rest for a couple of hours, or ideally, overnight in the fridge. Remove the meat from the refrigerator an hour before you plan to cook it.

2. When you're ready to make the curry, heat the oil or ghee in a heavy pan over a medium heat and add the bay leaves, cassia, cloves and cardamom pods. Fry for a minute to infuse the oil, then add the onions and ½ teaspoon of salt and cook for 10–12 minutes, until golden brown. (To save time, you can use 150g of fried brown onions along with a splash of water; see page 12.)

3. Add the ginger and garlic pastes and cook for a further 2 minutes, then add the marinated meat. Increase the heat to medium-high and cook, stirring constantly, until the meat begins to get some colour, 5–8 minutes.

4. Reduce the heat to low, add the chilli powder, cumin, coriander and garam masala and cook for a minute. Add the tomatoes and cook for 8–10 minutes, stirring occasionally, until they reduce to a thick paste and the fat begins to come to the surface.

5. Add the green chillies, jaggery, vinegar and 1 teaspoon of salt, along with 250–300ml of water. Give it all a mix, reduce the temperature to medium-low, cover and cook for 1 hour, stirring every 10–15 minutes.

6. Now transfer the curry to the oven. Preheat the oven to 150°C fan. If your pan is oven safe, cover with a lid or foil, or transfer the curry to a lidded casserole dish. Cook for 1–2 hours, checking on it every 20–30 minutes.

If at any point the meat begins to stick, reduce the temperature a bit and add a little more water. The exact cooking time will depend on the cut of meat, size of the chunks, thickness of the pan and the temperature you're cooking at. The key is not to rush it. Allowing the meat to cook slowly and break down fully will ensure that it retains its moisture and texture and yields the most delicious succulent curry. When you're happy with the consistency of the gravy and the texture of the meat, check the seasoning.

7. Serve garnished with fresh coriander and potato straws.

Goan Pork Vindaloo

Serves 4–6 as a main

*****

1kg pork belly or shoulder,
    boneless, skin trimmed,
    cut into 2.5–5cm pieces

1½ tsp salt

3 tbsp neutral oil

250g onions, thinly sliced

1 tsp jaggery or brown sugar

3 tbsp tomato purée, or 100g
    fresh tomatoes, finely chopped

*****

For the spice paste

5 dried Kashmiri or Byadgi red
    chillies, stems and seeds
    removed

2.5cm cassia bark or
    cinnamon stick

1 tsp black peppercorns

4 green cardamom pods

8 cloves

2 bay leaves

1 piece of mace, or a few gratings
    of nutmeg

½ tsp cumin seeds

4 garlic cloves, grated

2.5cm ginger, grated

60ml apple cider vinegar or white
    wine vinegar, to taste

No book on Indian cuisine would be complete without featuring this iconic dish from Goa. Renowned globally and a favourite at curry houses in the West, vindaloo has its origins in Portuguese cuisine. Goan cooks infused the traditional Portuguese dish with their own spices, creating the tangy, spice-laden vindaloo we know and love today. While it can be prepared with various meats, I think it's at its best when made with pork. If you can get your hands on some homemade Goan toddy or palm vinegar, be sure to use it here. A good vindaloo is a labour of love, and cooks in Goa meticulously prepare and cook it over a couple of days. I save this for weekends, preparing my spice paste and meat on a Saturday so it's ready to go into the oven in time for an unforgettable Sunday meal! Serve with pav or other crusty bread of your choice.

1. Start by making the spice paste. In a dry pan over a medium heat, toast the whole dry spices for about 2 minutes until they become aromatic. Transfer the toasted spices to a bowl and add the remaining spice paste ingredients. Mix well, then leave to soak for 2 hours.

2. After soaking, grind the spice mixture to a thick, smooth paste, using a grinder or blender.

3. Mix the pork pieces with the spice paste and ½ teaspoon of salt until well coated. Refrigerate the marinated pork for 3–4 hours, or preferably overnight. Take it out an hour before cooking to bring it to room temperature.

4. Heat the oil in a large pan (ovenproof, if you intend to transfer this to the oven later) over a medium heat. Add the onions and ½ teaspoon of salt, and cook until the onions turn light brown, about 6–8 minutes, then add the marinated pork to the pan along with the remaining salt, the jaggery and tomato purée. Fry for 10 minutes.

5. Meanwhile, if intending to transfer this to the oven, preheat the oven to 160°C fan.

6. Add 200ml of water to the pan, cover and cook in the oven for 2–3 hours until the meat is tender and falling apart. If you continue to cook it on the hob, it will take 1½–2 hours. Check the seasoning before serving.

Bihari One-Pot Meat Curry

Serves 4–6 as a main

*****

1.5kg lamb shoulder or neck,
    on the bone, cut into
    2.5–5cm pieces

1 tsp cumin seeds

250g onions, thinly sliced

8 garlic cloves, grated

5cm ginger, sliced

2 green chillies, slit lengthways

2 bay leaves

5 cloves

4 green cardamom pods

2 black cardamom pods

1 tbsp black peppercorns

1 piece of mace, or a few gratings
    of nutmeg

2.5cm cassia bark or
    cinnamon stick

1 tbsp Kashmiri red chilli powder

2 tbsp ground coriander

1 tbsp ground cumin

1 tsp kasoori methi (dried
    fenugreek leaves)

1 tsp garam masala (see
    page 267 for homemade)

1½ tsp salt

75ml mustard oil

1 whole head of garlic,
    top 1cm trimmed off to
    expose the cloves

This dish comes from the state of Bihar, where it's known as ahuna or Champaran meat. It's one of those unique recipes where everything is placed in a pot and cooked together, without the need to cook each ingredient individually or in sequence, and it all comes together wonderfully. The result is a beautiful, succulent meat curry packed with flavour. The key is to make sure that the cooking vessel is tightly sealed to create a pressured environment.

The repeated mention of garlic in the ingredient list is not a mistake. This recipe is heavy on garlic – cooking the whole head of garlic in oil imparts a wonderful flavour without overpowering the dish, while marinating the meat in grated garlic both tenderizes and flavours it. Traditionally, this dish is cooked over a fire in large covered earthen pots, sealed with a simple dough to create a tightly packed pressured environment. While I occasionally replicate this on the barbecue at home, I find the most consistent and failproof method is to cook it in a tightly sealed container in the oven. Serve with Fulkas (page 208), Parathas (page 216) or rice.

1. Place all the ingredients except half the mustard oil and the whole head of garlic in a large bowl and mix thoroughly. Leave to marinate at room temperature for an hour.

2. Preheat the oven to 150°C fan.

3. Heat the remaining mustard oil in a heavy, lidded, oven-safe pot over a high heat. When the oil begins to smoke, turn the heat off and swirl the oil to coat the entire pan. Place the whole head of garlic in the pan and pour the meat mix on top. Press it down gently so it's tightly packed. Place the lid on the pan and bake in the oven for 3 hours, stirring every hour.

4. Once the meat is tender, check the seasoning and serve.

Bengali Lamb Curry

Serves 4–6 as a main

*****

1.5kg lamb, mutton or goat
   shoulder or neck on the bone,
   cut into 2–5cm cubes

*****

For the marinade

1 tbsp garlic paste

1 tbsp ginger paste

1 tsp salt

1 green chilli, finely chopped

2 tbsp Greek-style yoghurt

½ tsp ground turmeric

½ tbsp Kashmiri red chilli powder

1 tbsp mustard oil

*****

For the curry

2 tbsp mustard oil

3 bay leaves

5cm cassia bark or cinnamon stick

3–5 cloves

3 dried red chillies

5 green cardamom pods

250g onions, finely sliced

½ tbsp ginger paste

½ tbsp garlic paste

1 tsp ground black pepper

1 tsp ground turmeric

1 tbsp Kashmiri red chilli powder

1½ tbsp ground coriander

1 tsp ground cumin

2 tbsp Greek-style yoghurt

1 tsp sugar

4 medium potatoes, peeled and
   roughly chopped

salt, to taste

green chillies, chopped, to garnish

Known as kosha mangsho in West Bengal, this is the quintessential Bengali meat curry, ideal for bringing out the best in tougher and cheaper cuts of meat. In India, it's traditionally made with goat meat, marinated for hours to tenderize it, then slow-cooked until it breaks down into a divine fall-off-the-bone curry. Often reserved for special occasions, it is a staple at Bengali weddings, auspicious occasions and family gatherings.

Selecting the right cut of meat is crucial. I prefer shoulder and neck on the bone, as these cuts yield the best results. Avoid using leg of lamb, as it tends to go dry with long, slow cooking.

Serve this glorious curry with plain rice or Luchis (see page 219). For an indulgent feast, pair it with Spicy Fried Aubergine (page 166) or Baked Mustard Fish (page 122). You can prepare this up to two days ahead, and reheat it in a pan or oven. It only gets better with time.

1. Mix together the ingredients for the marinade and rub them into the meat. Leave to rest for a couple of hours, or ideally overnight in the fridge.

2. Heat the mustard oil in a heavy pan over a medium heat. Add the bay leaves, cassia, cloves, chillies and cardamom pods, fry for a minute to infuse the oil, then add the onions and a pinch of salt. Cook for 10–12 minutes, until golden brown. (To save time, use 3 tablespoons of fried brown onions along with a splash of water – see page 12.)

3. Add the ginger and garlic pastes and cook for a further 2 minutes, then add the rest of the ground spices. Cook for a minute, then add the marinated meat. Increase the heat to medium-high and cook the meat, stirring constantly, until it begins to get some colour, about 5–8 minutes.

4. Take the pan off the heat and stir in the yoghurt along with the sugar, 1 teaspoon of salt and 350–400ml of water. Give it all a mix, then reduce the heat to medium-low, cover the pan and cook for 45 minutes–1 hour, stirring every 10–15 minutes.

NOTE: I often move the curry over to cook in the oven at this stage. It cooks a lot more evenly and needs less stirring. If your pot is oven-safe, put a lid or some foil on it and cook at 150°C fan for 1–2 hours, checking on it every 20–30 minutes. If at any point the meat begins to stick, reduce the temperature a bit and add a little water.

5. Remove the lid and add the potatoes 40 minutes before the end of the cooking time.

NOTE: The total cooking time will depend on the cut of meat, the size of the chunks, the thickness of the pan and the temperature you're cooking at. The key is not to rush it. Allowing the meat to cook slowly and break down fully will ensure that it retains its moisture and texture and yields the most delicious succulent curry.

6. When you're happy with the consistency of the gravy and the texture of the meat, check the seasoning and serve, garnished with green chillies.

Kerala Beef Ishtew

Serves 4–6 as a main

*****

2 tbsp coconut oil (or neutral
   vegetable oil)

5–6 green cardamom pods

5cm cinnamon stick

2 tsp black peppercorns

250g onions, thinly sliced

1½ tsp salt

1½ tbsp grated ginger

1½ tbsp grated garlic

8–10 curry leaves

1kg stewing beef, cut into chunks

1 large carrot, peeled and cut into
   2.5cm cubes

1 large potato, peeled and cut into
   2.5cm cubes

2 green chillies, slit lengthways

350ml coconut milk

½ tsp finely ground black pepper

1 tsp garam masala (optional)
   (see page 267 for homemade)

*****

For the seasoned oil

1 tbsp coconut oil

1 medium onion or 8–10 Thai
   shallots, thinly sliced

8–10 curry leaves

1 green chilli, slit lengthways
   (optional)

There's a common misconception that beef isn't used in Indian cooking. While goat (often referred to as lamb) is favoured in many regions, beef is very popular in certain parts of India, such as Goa and Kerala. In Kerala, leaner cuts are used in quick stir-fries, but most of the time, beef is slow-cooked or pressure-cooked into rich, succulent, melt-in-the-mouth curries. One such dish is the Kerala beef *ishtew* – an easy, wholesome, flavour-packed curry that's perfect for family meals and an excellent choice if you're new to cooking beef curries or favour something mild.

When preparing this dish, I ask my butcher for stewing beef cut into 4cm cubes, usually a mix of chuck, brisket and short rib. These cuts are more affordable, packed with connective tissue, and ideal for slow cooking, transforming into a deliciously tender and flavourful dish. If you're using bone-in cuts (which I highly recommend), increase the amount to 1.5kg to make sure there's plenty to go around. Serve with rice.

1. Heat the coconut oil in a deep pot over a medium heat. Add the cardamom pods, cinnamon, peppercorns and sliced onions with a pinch of salt and cook for 4–5 minutes until softened. The onions don't need to be browned for this curry, they just need to be soft and translucent.

2. Add the ginger, garlic and curry leaves and cook for a minute, then add the beef chunks and stir well to coat the meat with the spices and aromatics. Pour in enough water to just cover the beef, then cover and cook over a low simmer for 45 minutes–1 hour. You can cook the beef quicker in a pressure cooker, or put it into a slow cooker and let it stew until tender. I find the lower and longer you cook it for, the better the result. Skim off and discard any scum that rises to the surface.

3. Once the beef is tender, add the carrot, potato and chillies and cook uncovered for 10–12 minutes, adding a little more boiling water if required.

4. Stir in the coconut milk and simmer for another 8–10 minutes until the vegetables are fully cooked through. If you prefer a thicker curry, continue simmering over a medium heat for a few more minutes.

5. Sprinkle over the black pepper and garam masala (if using) and check the seasoning, then transfer the stew to a serving dish.

6. For the seasoned oil, heat the coconut oil in a small pan, add the onion or shallots and fry until golden brown. Add the curry leaves and green chilli (if using), fry for 15 seconds, then stir and pour over the stew before serving.

Sides

Potato Masala

Serves 4 as a side

*****

400g potatoes

2 tbsp neutral oil

½ tsp black mustard seeds

½ tsp asafoetida (optional)

2 tbsp raw cashew nuts, roughly
  chopped (optional)

½ tsp split yellow gram (optional)

200g onions, sliced

1 tsp grated ginger

1 green chilli, finely chopped

10–12 curry leaves

1 tsp ground turmeric

½ tsp salt, or to taste

juice of ½ lime

2 tbsp fresh coriander leaves,
  to garnish (optional)

This simple south Indian-style spiced potato side is most commonly used as a filling in dosas. Try some stuffed into a Semolina Dosa (page 40). It also shines when served as a side or as part of a larger feast. I often use leftovers in a Bombay Cheese Toastie (see page 27) instead of boiled potatoes, for an extra layer of flavour.

1. Boil the potatoes in their skins, then cool and peel. Boiling the potatoes in their skins ensures they don't soak up too much liquid, as this dish should be fairly dry. Once cool, coarsely mash the potatoes with a fork, ensuring that they maintain some texture.

2. Heat the oil in a pan over a medium heat. Add the mustard seeds and once they crackle, add the asafoetida, cashew nuts and lentils, if using. Cook for 30 seconds.

3. Add the onions and ginger, and cook until the onions have softened and turned translucent, but haven't started to turn golden.

4. Stir in the green chilli, curry leaves and turmeric and cook for 30 seconds.

5. Add the potatoes and salt and give it all a good mix. If the mixture seems too dry, add a splash of water. Check the seasoning and warm through over a medium heat for 3–4 minutes.

6. Squeeze the lime juice over the mixture and mix thoroughly before serving, garnished with coriander (if using).

Mustard Mashed Potatoes

Serves 4 as a side

*****

2½–3 tbsp salt, to taste

500g potatoes, peeled
   and quartered

1–2 tbsp mustard oil

120g red onions, finely chopped

2 tbsp finely chopped fresh
   coriander

1 green chilli, finely chopped

When diving deep into east Indian recipes a few years ago, a friend recommended I try aloo pitika, a popular dish from northeast India. At first glance, it didn't seem like much, but I'm still amazed at how a few simple ingredients can transform mashed potatoes into something extraordinary.

Once you've boiled some potatoes, this recipe can be whipped up in under five minutes – especially if your knife skills are sharp. For a twist, try swapping one potato for the flesh of a roasted aubergine. Check out my Burnt Aubergine Bharta recipe on page 44 for tips on roasting aubergines.

I've served these delicious potatoes as part of an Indian-inspired weekend roast featuring my Achari Traybake (page 137), with Simple Yellow Dal (page 75), or with Baked Mustard Fish (page 122). In Assamese homes, these are even eaten with plain rice – delicious, comforting carbs on carbs.

1. Fill a deep pan with 1.5–2 litres of water and add 2½ tablespoons of salt. Add the potatoes and bring the water to the boil over a high heat. Reduce the heat to medium and simmer for 20–30 minutes, until the potatoes are cooked through and tender. Drain and let them cool slightly.

2. In a mixing bowl, coarsely mash the warm potatoes. Drizzle in the mustard oil while mashing, adjusting the amount to your taste. I enjoy its pungent flavour and tend to be generous with it.

3. Add the remaining ingredients to the bowl and mix thoroughly with a spoon. Taste and adjust the seasoning as needed. Shape the potato mixture into small balls about the size of ping-pong balls. That's all there is to it! Serve warm or at room temperature if making this ahead.

Spicy Fried Aubergine

Serves 4 as a side

*****

2 large aubergines (approximately 700g total)

1 tbsp plus 1 tsp fine salt

2 tsp ground turmeric

2 tsp Kashmiri red chilli powder

2 tbsp granulated sugar

1½ tbsp plain flour

mustard oil, to fry

sea salt and lime wedges, to serve

I love aubergine, but just like okra, cabbage and cauliflower it needs to be prepared and cooked correctly for maximum impact. The best way to cook aubergine is to roast it over a high heat until brown on the outside, but still soft and custardy within. This recipe does just that, while taking it to the next level with the mustard oil and spicing.

This pan-fried aubergine dish, known as begun bhaja, is a staple in Bengali homes. I adore the contrasting textures of the soft custardy centre and the crisp caramelized exterior resulting from the sugar in the spice and flour dusting. It pairs brilliantly with Simple Yellow Dal (page 75) or Baked Mustard Fish (page 122) and some plain rice. If you don't have mustard oil, you can use a neutral oil, but you will miss out on some of the distinctive flavour.

If you want to make this dish gluten free, use gram flour or cornflour instead of plain flour.

1. Cut the aubergines into 1–1.5cm slices and lay them out on a chopping board or plate. Sprinkle with 1 tablespoon of fine salt, then flip and repeat. Leave them to rest for 8–10 minutes, then wipe them thoroughly with kitchen paper or a clean tea towel, removing as much of the salt and moisture as possible. This process seasons the aubergine slices and helps them to fry without absorbing too much oil.

2. Mix the turmeric, chilli powder, sugar and flour with 1 teaspoon of fine salt in a bowl. Coat the aubergine slices on each side with this dry rub. You might need to dip each side a couple of times to get an even coating.

3. In a large frying pan set over a medium-high heat, warm enough oil to pan-fry the aubergines in batches. Spread the slices out and fry for 2–3 minutes on each side. You want them crisp and golden on the outside and fully cooked through on the inside. You may need to flip them a few more times and add more oil, depending on the size and thickness of your pan and the cooking temperature.

4. Once fully cooked, serve and enjoy immediately, perhaps with another sprinkle of sea salt and some lime wedges for squeezing.

Okra Pachadi

Serves 4 as a side

✻✻✻✻✻

250g okra

1½ tsp fine salt, to taste

1 tbsp cumin seeds

50g desiccated coconut

1 green chilli

2½ tbsp coconut oil

1 tsp black mustard seeds

10–12 curry leaves

½ tsp ground turmeric

½ tsp asafoetida

250g natural or Greek-style
   yoghurt

1 dried red chilli, stem and
   seeds removed

This south Indian yoghurt-based side dish is one of my favourite ways to cook okra. It is incredibly versatile, and works equally well with cucumber, beetroot, pineapple or pumpkin. You'll need to adapt the cooking times and methods to suit the vegetable you choose.

   The next time you cook a biryani, try serving a pachadi instead of a raita. Alternatively, it's fantastic as part of a light meal alongside some plain rice and protein of your choice.

1. Wash the okra and dry thoroughly. Cut the tops off and slice them widthways into 1cm slices, then place in a bowl and sprinkle over 1 teaspoon of the salt. Mix well and set aside.

2. Toast the cumin seeds in a dry pan set over a medium heat until they begin to smell aromatic and turn a slightly darker brown. Be careful not to burn them. Set aside.

3. Soak the desiccated coconut in 200ml warm water for 2-3 minutes, then drain well, squeezing out any excess water with your hands. Transfer to a pestle and mortar or spice grinder and coarsely grind along with the green chilli and cumin seeds.

4. Heat 1½ tablespoons of the coconut oil in a pan over a medium heat and add half the mustard seeds. Once they crackle, add the okra and half the curry leaves. Stir-fry for 2–3 minutes, then add the turmeric and asafoetida and cook for a minute longer. Add the coconut mixture and cook for another 2–3 minutes.

5. Mix the yoghurt with 100ml of water and the remaining ½ teaspoon of salt and add it to the cooked okra. Remove from the heat and mix thoroughly. You can prepare this up to a day ahead and keep it refrigerated.

6. Before serving, heat the remaining tablespoon of coconut oil in a small pan and add the rest of the mustard seeds, the remaining curry leaves and the dried chilli. Once the mustard seeds stop crackling, pour it all over the pachadi and stir through. You can serve this chilled or at room temperature.

Raita

Serves 4–6 as a side

*****

400g natural yoghurt

200g cucumber, peeled, seeds removed, finely chopped

50g red onion, finely chopped (optional)

1 green chilli, finely chopped (optional)

½ tsp toasted cumin seeds, coarsely ground

½ tsp salt, or to taste

½ tsp ground black pepper

½ tsp sugar (optional)

½ tsp Kashmiri red chilli powder

½ tsp chaat masala (see page 266 for homemade)

2 tbsp finely chopped fresh coriander leaves

A classic side on most Indian menus, this dish is particularly popular served alongside biryanis or Punjabi home-style meals. At its simplest, a raita is no more than lightly seasoned yoghurt with a sprinkling of roasted cumin seeds and chopped vegetables such as onions, cucumber or tomatoes. However, more elaborate versions can include fresh pomegranate seeds, spiced pineapple, burnt aubergine, crunchy gram flour balls (known as boondi) and much more.

1. In a large mixing bowl, whisk the yoghurt until smooth and creamy.

2. Add the remaining ingredients, saving a pinch each of the Kashmiri chilli powder, chaat masala and fresh coriander, to garnish the dish. Mix everything together until well combined. Taste and adjust the seasoning, if necessary.

3. Chill the raita in the fridge before serving.

4. When ready to serve, garnish with the reserved Kashmiri chilli powder, chaat masala and fresh coriander.

Masala Papad

Makes 4 x 15cm papads

*****

4 raw black pepper papads,
   or packaged fried papads

1 large fresh tomato, seeds
   removed and flesh
   finely chopped

100g red onions, finely chopped

2 tbsp finely chopped fresh
   coriander leaves

2 green chillies, finely chopped

*****

For the chilli oil tarka

2 tbsp butter or neutral oil

1 tsp cumin seeds

1 tsp Kashmiri red chilli powder

1 tsp chaat masala (see page 266
   for homemade), plus extra
   to sprinkle

Masala papads always bring back memories of evenings watching cricket matches with friends and family in Mumbai, all gathered around the television, sipping beers, and munching on a variety of savoury snacks. These were a staple and would disappear almost as quickly as they were brought out of the kitchen.

The cooking method for papads varies, based on the variety used. South Indian papads usually require deep-frying, while north Indian papads can be fried, roasted, toasted in a dry pan, or even cooked in the microwave. My favourite is the Sindhi or Punjabi papad, made from milled black lentils and black pepper, commonly labelled as 'black pepper urid papad'. If raw papads are hard to find, you can use the fried ones commonly found at most large supermarkets.

Prepare the toppings ahead of time and store them in the fridge, so you can quickly assemble these in time for kick-off. Serve them alongside a chilled beer or fresh lime soda.

1. If using raw papads, cook them in one of the following ways:

Direct flame: Hold a papad with tongs and roast it directly over a low flame. Keep flipping and moving it around quickly to make sure it cooks evenly and doesn't burn. It will begin to bubble up and char in places. Transfer to a serving plate when evenly cooked. This method works best for those with a gas hob.

Dry pan: Heat a large dry pan over a medium-high heat. Place a papad on it and gently press it down with a spatula or tea towel. Flip once and transfer to a serving plate when evenly cooked.

Oven or air fryer: Place the papads on a preheated baking tray and roast in the oven at 180°C fan, or place in the air fryer at 180°C, for 3–4 minutes. Once evenly cooked, transfer to a serving plate.

Microwave: Cook the papads one at a time for 30–60 seconds on full power, in short bursts of 10 seconds. Once evenly cooked, transfer to a serving plate.

2. After you have cooked the papads, make the chilli oil. Heat the butter or oil in a small pan over a medium heat. Add the cumin seeds, and once they crackle, take the pan off the heat. Add the chilli powder and chaat masala

to the hot oil and mix thoroughly, cooking them in the residual heat for 30 seconds. Brush or spoon this oil evenly over the papads.

3. Top each oiled papad with the tomatoes, onions, coriander and green chillies. Sprinkle with some more chaat masala and serve immediately. You can cook the papads and make the chilli oil ahead of time, but don't assemble them until just before serving, to prevent them getting soggy.

Kachumber

Serves 4 as a side

*****

220–250g ripe tomato, seeds
  removed, finely chopped

250–300g cucumber,
  finely chopped

100g red onions, finely chopped

3–4 tbsp finely chopped fresh
  coriander leaves

1 green chilli, finely chopped
  (optional)

1 tsp toasted cumin seeds,
  coarsely ground

½ tsp coarsely ground
  black pepper

1 tsp chaat masala (see page 266
  for homemade)

1 tbsp lemon or lime juice

¼ tsp salt, to taste

Salads aren't very common in traditional Indian cookery. Presumably this is because of the tropical climate and an inherent suspicion of anything uncooked in those conditions. The kachumber is probably the closest you'll come to what's seen as a salad in the West. It's a very simple dish, where each element is optional or replaceable based on preference and availability. We make versions of this at home very often. I think the combination of toasted ground cumin, lime juice and black pepper makes such a fantastic dressing.

1. In a large mixing bowl, combine the finely chopped tomato, cucumber, red onion, coriander leaves and green chilli, if using. Mix everything together gently.

2. Sprinkle the cumin, black pepper, chaat masala, lemon or lime juice and salt over the chopped vegetables, and toss everything together to ensure the spices are evenly distributed.

3. Taste and adjust the seasoning if necessary. Serve immediately.

Lachcha Onions

Serves 4 as a side

*****

250–300g red onions, sliced into 5mm rings

½ tsp salt

1 tsp chaat masala (see page 266 for homemade)

½ tsp Kashmiri red chilli powder

1 tbsp lemon or lime juice

2 tbsp finely chopped fresh coriander leaves

Raw onions are often passed off as a 'salad' in India and are eaten in abundant quantities at mealtimes across India. These dressed onions are slightly fancier, are simple to put together and make for a great accompaniment or garnish for kebabs and tandoori dishes. If you fear the after-effects of eating raw onions on your breath and social life, try soaking the sliced onions in iced water for about 10 minutes before draining and serving them. I find this significantly reduces their pungency and the unpleasant after-taste.

1. Separate the onion rings and place them in a large mixing bowl. Cover with ice-cold water and allow to sit for 5 minutes. Then drain and dry the onions thoroughly and return them to a dry mixing bowl.

2. Sprinkle the salt, chaat masala, Kashmiri red chilli powder and lemon or lime juice over the onions, then toss everything together until the onions are evenly coated with the spices and lemon juice.

3. Garnish with fresh coriander and give the onions one final toss before serving.

Lemon Pickle

Makes about 500g

*****

250g unwaxed lemons

15–20g salt, to taste

100ml apple cider vinegar, or
white wine vinegar

½ tsp black mustard seeds

½ tsp fenugreek seeds

100ml neutral oil

1 green chilli, cut into 2cm pieces

½ tsp asafoetida

2 tsp sugar

½ tsp ground turmeric

2 tbsp Kashmiri red chilli powder

My friend Renjith (also our executive chef at Hoppers) is one of the most gifted pickle-makers I know. We often joke about starting a pickle business together when we retire. This recipe is an adaptation of his classic South Indian lime pickle.

In India, pickles are just as much about preserving ingredients as they are about adding layer upon layer of flavour to them. At mealtimes, we often bring out a variety of pickles and chutneys, and just a spoonful or two can punctuate the meal with intense bursts of flavour between bites.

This lemon pickle is my go-to accompaniment to Yoghurt and Cucumber Rice (page 196). As unusual as it might sound, the combination of the crunchy, cooling rice with this zingy pickle is a match made in heaven.

1. Slice the lemons into 2.5mm thick rings or half-moons, and put them into a clean mixing bowl. Make sure you collect all the juices and add them to the bowl. Sprinkle 1 tablespoon of salt and 2 tablespoons of vinegar over the lemons and mix well. Cover and store in the fridge for 5–10 days, stirring the contents once a day.

2. In the meantime, combine the mustard seeds and fenugreek seeds and either crush them to a coarse powder in a pestle and mortar or pulse them a few times in a spice grinder.

3. Heat the oil in a small wok or pan over a medium heat. Add the green chilli and asafoetida and cook for 30 seconds.

4. Take the pan off the heat and add the ground mustard/fenugreek, sugar, turmeric, Kashmiri chilli powder and the remaining salt. Stir well and return the pan to the heat. Instantly add the lemons, along with any juice in the bowl, and the vinegar. Cook over a low heat until some of the liquid evaporates and the spiced red oil rises to the top – about 8–10 minutes.

5. Taste for seasoning and balance, adding more salt or sugar if necessary. Cook for a final minute, then transfer the hot pickle to a clean airtight glass or ceramic jar. It's better not to use plastic containers or reactive metal jars to store pickles.

6. Allow the pickle to mature at room temperature in the jar for two days before tucking in. After two days, keep it refrigerated but bring it to room temperature before serving.

Green Chilli Thecha

Makes about 200g

*****

100g green chillies

1 tbsp neutral oil

1 tsp cumin seeds

20g garlic, roughly chopped

30g peanuts, roasted and husked

40g fresh coriander leaves

½ tsp salt, to taste

1½ tbsp apple cider vinegar,
  or white wine vinegar

A staple in Maharashtrian homes in the west, this is more a fresh green chilli relish than a pickle. Akin to a fiery green chutney, but a lot coarser in texture, it's a wonderful little side to elevate even a simple meal of dal and rice. And the best bit is that it takes less than five minutes to put together.

   While you can use a blender or food processor to make thecha, I find it is best hand pounded in a pestle and mortar. The action of pounding breaks down the ingredients and releases flavour in a way that the chopping action of a food processor cannot replicate.

   Serve this alongside everything from a simple meal of dal and rice to a full-blown feast.

1. Wash the green chillies and dry them thoroughly. Remove the stems and roughly chop the chillies.

2. Heat the oil in a pan over a medium-high heat. Add the cumin seeds and let them sizzle for a few seconds.

3. Add the chopped green chillies to the pan and cook for 2–3 minutes, until they soften slightly and char in spots.

4. Remove the pan from the heat. Let the mixture cool for a few minutes.

5. Combine the fried chillies and cumin, garlic, roasted peanuts, coriander leaves and salt. Crush to a coarse texture in a pestle and mortar, or pulse them a few times in a spice grinder. Avoid making a smooth paste – the texture should be chunky. Add the vinegar and check the seasoning, adjusting the salt and vinegar to your taste.

6. Transfer the thecha to a clean, dry jar and store it in the fridge. It can be kept for up to a week.

Carrot Pickle

Makes about 500g

*****

350g carrots, peeled and cut into
   5cm sticks

1 tbsp salt

1 tbsp yellow or black mustard
   seeds

1 tsp fenugreek seeds

1 tsp fennel seeds

75ml mustard oil, or any neutral oil

1 tsp nigella seeds

¼ tsp asafoetida

1 tsp ground turmeric

1 tsp Kashmiri red chilli powder
   (optional)

50g green chillies, slit (optional)

50ml apple cider vinegar, or white
   wine vinegar

Pickles are regularly served as condiments at Indian meals. Yet again, each region has its unique style and variations. Gujaratis favour sweeter pickles, while sour lime pickles are a hit in the south. This Punjabi-style carrot pickle from the north is more about packing the simple carrot with flavour than preserving it. Once you've tried this recipe, feel free to replace the carrots with other vegetables, such as radishes, turnips, green mangoes, fresh chillies and even raw cauliflower.

1. Place the carrots in a large mixing bowl, sprinkle over the salt and mix well. Cover and let them sit for 2 hours. This will draw out excess moisture.

2. After 2 hours, drain the water released from the carrots and spread them on a tray lined with kitchen paper to dry for another 2–3 hours.

3. In the meantime, heat a dry pan over a medium heat and toast the mustard, fenugreek and fennel seeds for 2 minutes. Allow them to cool completely, then crush to a coarse powder in a pestle and mortar or pulse them a few times in a spice grinder.

4. Heat the mustard oil in a small pan over a medium heat until it starts to smoke. Turn off the heat and let it cool slightly for a couple of minutes.

5. In a mixing bowl, combine the crushed spice mix, nigella seeds, asafoetida, turmeric and chilli powder (if using). Add the mustard oil to the spice mixture and stir well. The oil should be still warm but not hot enough to burn the spices.

6. Add the dried carrot sticks and green chillies (if using) and mix well to coat them evenly with the spice and oil mixture. Add the vinegar and mix well.

7. Transfer the pickle to a clean, dry, airtight glass or ceramic jar. It's better not to use plastic containers or reactive metal jars to store pickles. Seal the jar and let the pickle sit at room temperature in a sunny place for 3–4 days to mature, shaking the jar gently once a day to redistribute the spices.

8. The pickle will be ready to eat after 3–4 days. You can store the jar in the fridge to keep the pickle fresh for up to a month.

Simple Green Chutney

Makes about 200g

*****

100g fresh coriander, leaves
  and stems

30g fresh mint leaves

2 green chillies

2.5cm ginger, peeled

juice of 1 lime, or more to taste

1 tsp toasted cumin seeds,
  coarsely ground

½ tsp chaat masala (see page 266
  for homemade)

1 tsp sugar, or more to taste

½ tsp salt

This simple green chutney is incredibly versatile and pairs well with a variety of snacks. For chaats, I usually skip the garlic, but if you're serving it with kebabs, feel free to add a clove or two. I prefer my chutney spicy with a hint of sweetness, but you can easily adjust the chillies and sugar to suit your taste.

Pictured with Coconut and Peanut Chutney (page 189) and Tangy Tamarind Chutney (page 188).

1. Blend all the ingredients together to form a bright green paste, adding up to 50ml of water if necessary. Adjust the seasoning to your taste, adding a little more sugar or salt as required.

2. Store refrigerated in an airtight container for up to 3 days or freeze immediately, to retain the chutney's brightness.

Tangy Tamarind Chutney

Makes 500g

*****

150g dried tamarind

150g pitted dates

1 tsp roasted cumin seeds

1 tsp Kashmiri red chilli powder

1 tsp ground ginger

150g jaggery (or brown sugar),
   or more to taste

1 tsp salt

While you can find excellent store-bought versions of tamarind chutney, preparing it at home allows you to tailor the contrasting flavours to your personal preference. This condiment is fantastic alongside fried snacks like samosas and bhajias, inside vada pavs or drizzled over chaats. I make this using dried tamarind, which I soak in warm water, squeeze to a pulp, and strain to remove any seeds and husk. Pre-made tamarind pastes often contain additives like sugar and salt, and vary in concentration, so it's best to use pure dried tamarind if you decide to make this chutney at home.

1. Begin by preparing the tamarind pulp. Soak the tamarind block in 150ml of boiling water for about 15 minutes. Squeeze the tamarind well to extract all the juice, then strain through a sieve to remove any seeds and fibres.

2. Combine all the ingredients in a saucepan over a medium heat and add about 400ml of water. Bring to the boil, then reduce the heat to the lowest setting and simmer for 12–15 minutes until the dates have completely softened and the mixture has thickened.

3. Allow it to cool completely, then blend to a thick paste, adding a splash of water if needed.

4. Check the seasoning and add more salt or jaggery, if required, mixing thoroughly to make sure they have dissolved.

5. Store refrigerated in an airtight container for up to 1 week, or freeze immediately.

Coconut and Peanut Chutney

Makes about 200g

*****

For the chutney base

200g coconut, grated, ideally
    fresh, or frozen

100g roasted unsalted peanuts

2.5cm ginger, peeled

1 green chilli, seeds removed

*****

For the spiced oil

2 tbsp neutral oil

1 tsp black mustard seeds

½ tsp asafoetida

10 curry leaves

2 dried red chillies, seeds removed

Coconut chutney is a classic south Indian side and is essential alongside dosas and idlis. Traditionally it is made with roasted gram, but as that's not the easiest ingredient to source, I often turn to roasted unsalted peanuts instead. Not only are peanuts a great substitute, but they also add a wonderful depth to the dish.

1. Grind all the ingredients for the chutney base in a blender, adding water as required to achieve the consistency you like. I like my chutney smooth and fairly thick, but I know people who prefer it very runny. Season once you're done blending, then transfer the chutney to a serving bowl.

2. In a small pan, heat the oil over a medium heat. Once hot, add the mustard seeds. When they begin to crackle, add the asafoetida, curry leaves and red chillies. Fry for 30 seconds, then pour the oil and spices over the chutney. Stir well and serve immediately.

3. You can make this chutney ahead and serve it chilled, if you like. Store refrigerated in an airtight container for up to 3 days or freeze immediately.

RICE

Lemon Rice

Makes about 500g

* * * * *

400–500g cooked basmati rice
(see page 270)

* * * * *

For the lemon mix

2 tablespoons neutral oil

6 tbsp skin-on peanuts, or raw
cashews (optional)

1 tsp black mustard seeds

1 tsp split white lentils

1 tbsp grated ginger

3 dried red chillies, stems
removed but left whole

¼ tsp asafoetida (optional)

1½ tsp ground turmeric

10–12 curry leaves

60ml freshly squeezed lemon
juice

1 tsp salt

This south Indian recipe is a great way to use up leftover rice. You can make up a big batch of the lemon mix and store it in an airtight container in the fridge for up to a week. Mix it with some cooked rice whenever you like and serve hot or cold.

This refreshing dish needs nothing more than a light curry or a Pachadi (page 169) to go with it.

1. Heat 1 tablespoon of oil in a pan set over a medium heat. If using nuts, add them to the pan and fry until they turn a shade darker, about 2 minutes. Transfer the nuts to a plate lined with kitchen paper.

2. Add the remaining oil to the pan and, once hot, add the mustard seeds. When the seeds start to crackle, add the split white lentils and cook for a minute. When the mustard seeds stop crackling and the lentils turn light brown, reduce the heat to low and add the ginger, chillies, asafoetida, turmeric and curry leaves. Cook for a minute, then remove from the heat. Allow to cool for 5 minutes.

3. Stir in the lemon juice, fried nuts (if using) and salt. Mix thoroughly and rest for 5–10 minutes. The lemon mix is now ready and can be used immediately or refrigerated in an airtight container for up to a week.

4. To make lemon rice, simply mix the lemon mix with some freshly cooked or reheated basmati rice. The entire batch of lemon mix is good for about 500g of cooked rice, but you can adjust the quantity proportionately, as needed.

Tamarind and Peanut Rice

Makes about 500g

*****

400–500g cooked basmati rice
  (see page 270)

*****

For the spice powder

1 tbsp white sesame seeds

2 tbsp unsalted peanuts

1 tsp fenugreek seeds

a large pinch of asafoetida

*****

For the tamarind mix

2 tbsp neutral oil

6 tbsp peanuts (ideally skin on)

1 tsp black mustard seeds

1 tbsp grated ginger

1 tsp ground turmeric

10–15 curry leaves

1 tbsp Kashmiri red chilli powder

1½ tbsp tamarind pulp
  (see page 188)

1½ tbsp jaggery, or brown sugar

1 tsp salt

Tamarind rice is one of the first south Indian dishes I remember eating. My grand-uncle Tatun would cook this for us and serve it with a variety of curries, stir-fries and pachadis.

The savoury spice mix cooked with tamarind pulp gives the rice an incredible nutty depth of flavour. Often, when in the mood for a light, quick and nostalgic meal, I make this simple dish and eat it with a big bowl of chilled yoghurt and pickle. Add a light sambhar or dal for a truly comforting meal.

1. Start by making the spice powder. Toast all the ingredients in a dry pan for 2–3 minutes over a medium-low heat until aromatic. Transfer to a plate to cool, then grind to a coarse powder in a pestle and mortar or a spice grinder.

2. For the tamarind mix, heat 1 tablespoon of oil in a pan set over a medium heat, then add the peanuts and fry until they darken in colour, about 2 minutes. Remove to a plate lined with kitchen paper. Add the remaining tablespoon of oil to the pan and once hot, add the mustard seeds.

3. When the mustard seeds stop crackling, add the ginger, turmeric and curry leaves and cook for 30 seconds.

4. Reduce the temperature to low. Add the spice mix and the Kashmiri chilli powder and cook for 2 minutes, being careful not to let it burn. Add the tamarind pulp, jaggery, salt and 200ml of water. Simmer over a medium-low heat until reduced to a third and thick and glossy, about 5–6 minutes. The tamarind mix is now ready and can be used immediately, or refrigerated in an airtight container for up to a week.

5. To make tamarind rice, simply mix the tamarind mix with some freshly cooked or reheated basmati rice. The entire batch of tamarind mix is good for about 500g of cooked rice, but you can adjust the quantity proportionately, as needed.

Yoghurt and Cucumber Rice

Serves 4–6

*****

400–500g cooked basmati
   rice (see page 270), chilled

1 large cucumber, peeled and
   finely chopped

300g natural yoghurt

1 tsp salt

sugar, to taste

*****

For the spiced oil

4 tbsp neutral oil

1 tsp black mustard seeds

1 tsp split white lentils, or
   unsalted peanuts

1 tbsp grated ginger

2 green chillies, finely chopped

½ tsp asafoetida (optional)

10–12 curry leaves

Curd rice, as we call this dish in India, is my go-to dish for a light, cold supper on hot summer evenings. This five-minute dish is an ideal way to use up leftover rice, particularly rice that's been overcooked and has gone mushy. Frying white lentils adds a beautiful nuttiness and great crunch to the dish, but if you can't find white lentils, any kind of nuts, especially peanuts, make a good substitute. Asafoetida is readily available in large supermarkets or online.

Eating cold rice gets a hard time, but it's a common practice in India. Something done frequently, with little thought and no injury. To use cold rice safely, cool your rice as quickly as possible after cooking by spreading it in trays or stirring it in large bowls. Don't let it hang around at room temperature. Once cooled, pack it into an airtight container and refrigerate immediately. Eat within a day or two. The rice doesn't need to be reheated, just remove it from the fridge 20–30 minutes before serving.

1. Combine the rice, cucumber, yoghurt and salt in a bowl and mix well. Adjust the consistency with water until it resembles a thick rice pudding. If the yoghurt is too sour, add a touch of sugar to balance it. I prefer it slightly sour. Transfer the mixture to a serving bowl and set aside.

2. Heat 2 tablespoons of oil in a pan set over a medium heat and once hot, add the mustard seeds. When the seeds start to crackle, add the split white lentils and cook for a minute.

3. When the mustard seeds stop crackling and the lentils turn light brown, reduce the heat to low and add the ginger, green chillies, asafoetida and curry leaves. Cook for a minute, then pour over the rice and serve immediately. The spiced oil over the rice makes a beautiful garnish, but be sure to stir it through the rice thoroughly before serving.

4. Enjoy this dish simply with a tangy south Indian lemon pickle (page 180) on the side.

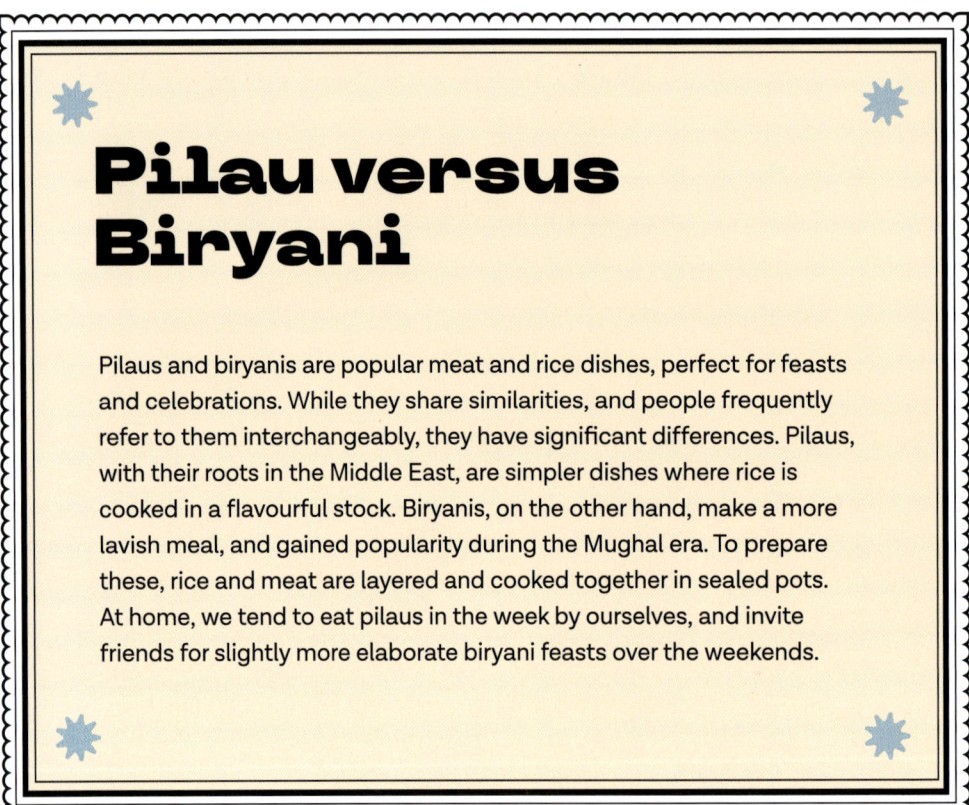

Pilau versus Biryani

Pilaus and biryanis are popular meat and rice dishes, perfect for feasts and celebrations. While they share similarities, and people frequently refer to them interchangeably, they have significant differences. Pilaus, with their roots in the Middle East, are simpler dishes where rice is cooked in a flavourful stock. Biryanis, on the other hand, make a more lavish meal, and gained popularity during the Mughal era. To prepare these, rice and meat are layered and cooked together in sealed pots. At home, we tend to eat pilaus in the week by ourselves, and invite friends for slightly more elaborate biryani feasts over the weekends.

Chicken Pilau

Serves 6–8

*****

For the chicken stock

1kg chicken legs, skinless but on the bone, cut into 5–8cm pieces

1 medium onion, peeled and cut into quarters

1 head of garlic, left whole

5cm ginger

2 bay leaves

8cm cassia bark, or cinnamon stick

*****

My mother-in-law has a magic touch when it comes to pilaus, often transforming leftover meat or chicken curries into a delicious meal the day after a big dinner party. Her pilaus are so good that I always cook extra when entertaining and send her the leftover curries to turn into a flavour-packed pilau.

   This is her recipe for a simple, yet very comforting chicken pilau made from scratch. We eat a version of this at least once a week at home, accompanied simply by some green chillies and a bowl of thick Greek yoghurt topped with a sprinkling of chaat masala.

   If you're looking to repurpose a leftover curry, separate the curry and meat and run the curry down to a thin watery sauce. Then follow the recipe opposite, skipping steps 1 and 3, and substituting the stock with your curry and the boiled chicken with the strained meat.

For the spice bag

6 cloves

6 green cardamom pods

3 black cardamom pods

2 tsp black peppercorns

1 tsp fennel seeds

1 tbsp coriander seeds

*****

For the rice

500g raw basmati rice

2 tbsp ghee or butter

1 tsp cumin seeds

1 tsp black peppercorns

2 green cardamom pods

1 black cardamom

1 large onion, thinly sliced

2 tbsp Greek-style yoghurt

1 green chilli, slit

2 tsp salt, to taste

*****

For the garnish

1 tbsp fresh mint leaves

1 tbsp chopped fresh coriander
   leaves

5cm ginger, cut into matchsticks

1. Begin by making the chicken stock. Tie all the ingredients for the spice bag in a small piece of muslin cloth or cheesecloth and place it in a deep saucepan along with all the stock ingredients and 2 litres of water. Cover and bring to a gentle boil over a medium heat, then lower the temperature and let it gently simmer, covered, for 45 minutes. Turn off the heat and set aside for a few minutes while you get on with the rice.

2. Place the rice in a bowl and wash with several rounds of cold water, gently swirling it with your hands until the water runs somewhat clear. Cover with fresh water and leave to soak for 30 minutes.

3. While the rice is soaking, strain the stock, discarding any whole spices and the spice bag. Using tongs, transfer the chicken pieces to a bowl and set aside. Press the onion, garlic and ginger with the back of a spoon, extracting as much pulp as possible. Discard the skins and the rest of the solids. Set the strained stock aside.

4. To make the pilau, drain the rice and discard the water. Heat the ghee in a deep pan over a medium heat. Add the cumin seeds, peppercorns and both types of cardamom and fry for 30 seconds. Add the onion and fry until deeply caramelized, about 10–12 minutes. You can use 2 tablespoons of brown onions and a splash of water to save time here (see page 12).

5. Remove the pan from the heat briefly and stir in the yoghurt and green chilli. Then return it to a low heat and add the soaked and drained rice. Cook for 2 minutes, then add 750ml of the chicken stock, 2 teaspoons of salt and the chicken pieces. Freeze any leftover stock or use it in other curries.

6. Increase the heat to high, bring everything to the boil, and cook until the water level drops to the level of the rice, about 3 minutes. Then reduce the heat to low, cover the pan with a tight-fitting lid or tin foil and continue to cook for 20 minutes. Turn off the heat and rest the pilau for 5 minutes, then remove the lid and gently fluff up the rice with a fork.

7. Garnish the pilau with mint, coriander and ginger and serve immediately.

Easy Chicken Biryani

Serves 4–6

*****

400–500g cooked basmati rice

*****

For the brown onions

neutral oil, to deep-fry

500g onions, thinly sliced

*****

For the chicken curry

1kg chicken, skinless, on the bone,
  cut into 5cm pieces

120g natural yoghurt

1 tsp ground turmeric

1 tsp salt

1½ tsp ginger paste

1½ tsp garlic paste

2 tbsp ghee or neutral oil

1 tbsp Kashmiri red chilli powder

250g tomatoes, finely chopped (or
  200g tinned chopped tomatoes)

2 tbsp biryani masala, homemade
  or store-bought

1 green chilli, slit lengthways

juice of ½ lemon or lime

*****

For the rice

400g basmati rice

1 cinnamon stick

4 green cardamom pods

4 cloves

2 bay leaves

salt, to taste

*****

To assemble and garnish

3 tbsp each chopped fresh
  coriander and mint leaves

1 tbsp kewra or rose water

a pinch of saffron, soaked in
  2 tbsp warm milk (optional)

1 tbsp ghee

I was once asked on a podcast what my desert island dish would be. Without hesitation, my response was 'biryani'. The definitive one-pot meal, biryanis have it all – protein, carbs, herbs, nuts, spices, texture and a whole lot of flavour. Understandably, they can seem intimidating to make, but follow a few simple tips and you'll be assembling these in minutes and casually giving your dinner party guests the impression you've slaved for hours in the kitchen putting it all together.

1. Start with the brown onions. Heat the oil in a wok to about 170–180°C. Test the oil temperature by dropping a single onion slice into the oil. If it sizzles and comes to the surface rapidly, the oil is ready. Add the onion slices in batches. Don't overcrowd the pan, as this can lower the oil temperature and result in soggy onions. Fry, stirring occasionally with a slotted spoon, until the onions are golden brown and crisp. This usually takes about 7–10 minutes, depending on the thickness of the slices. Remove with a slotted spoon to drain on a plate lined with kitchen paper. (If you're uncomfortable with deep-frying, fry the onions in smaller batches in a shallow pan, with enough oil to ensure they brown well and crisp up.)

2. Next, marinate the chicken. In a bowl, combine the chicken pieces with the yoghurt, turmeric, ½ teaspoon of salt, a third of the browned onions and ½ teaspoon each of ginger and garlic pastes. Mix well and let the chicken marinate for an hour, or better still, overnight.

3. Prepare the rice. Wash the rice under cold water until the water runs somewhat clear, then soak the rice in fresh water for 30 minutes and drain.

4. In a large pot, bring 2 litres of water to the boil. Add the cinnamon, cardamom, cloves, bay leaves, 2 teaspoons of salt and the soaked and drained rice, and cook until the rice is 70% done, about 7–8 minutes. Test by squeezing a grain; it should be cooked on the outside but slightly hard in the centre. Drain the rice immediately and spread it out on a large tray to prevent overcooking.

5. Cook the chicken. Heat the ghee or oil in a large, heavy pan over a medium-high heat. Add the remaining ginger and garlic pastes and cook for 30 seconds until fragrant, then add the marinated chicken and the

Kashmiri chilli powder to the pan and cook for 4–6 minutes, until the chicken is evenly browned.

6. Add the tomatoes and biryani masala, cover and cook for 6–8 minutes.

7. Remove the pan from the heat, add the green chilli and squeeze in the lemon or lime juice. Mix well and allow the curry to cool slightly before layering.

8. To layer the biryani, sprinkle half of the remaining brown onions, and half of the coriander and mint leaves over the chicken curry. Layer the rice over the chicken curry, then top with the remaining brown onions, the rest of the coriander and mint leaves, kewra or rose water and the saffron milk (if using). Drizzle the ghee down the sides of the rice.

9. Cover the pot with a tight-fitting lid or a double layer of tin foil and cook over a low heat for 20–25 minutes. This allows the rice and meat to steam together and cook completely.

10. Turn off the heat and leave to rest for 10 minutes before opening the lid. You can make this up to a couple of hours ahead, just keep the lid on tightly and keep warm in a very low oven. Serve with a raita of your choice.

Notes

- Always keep a container of fried onions to hand. These can be time-consuming to make, but they last ages and are extremely versatile (see page 12).
- Store-bought biryani masala is just as effective as homemade, and a lot quicker. If you are making it from scratch, be sure to make a large batch and store any excess in an airtight jar. It will save you a lot of time next time you make a biryani, which might be sooner than you think.
- When serving biryani, keep it simple. Avoid too many sides. A raita and a simple salad of sliced tomatoes, onions, cucumbers and green chillies with a sprinkling of chaat masala does the trick for me. If you really want to indulge, go ahead and serve some kebabs as a starter. Serving curries and rich sides distracts from the biryani and ends up overwhelming the plate and palate.

BREADS

Fulkas

Makes 6–7

*****

130g chapati flour, plus extra
   for rolling

1 tsp neutral oil or 5g ghee

¼ tsp salt

extra ghee or butter, to garnish
   (optional)

Having lived away from India for nearly two decades, few indulgences compare to the joy of a freshly cooked, puffy fulka (aka roti, rotli, poli or chapati) landing on your plate just as you've finished the previous one.

   This unleavened whole-wheat bread is one of the simplest and most commonly eaten breads across the nation. Despite its apparent simplicity, I struggled for years to perfect the recipe. This deviates from traditional recipes, but delivers a consistent result from the very first attempt.

1. Place the flour in a mixing bowl and add 80ml warm water. Bring together with a fork, then mix with your fingers until you see no dry bits of flour. You don't need to knead the dough; you're just bringing it together. You may need to add another 10ml warm water to help it come together. Cover with a tea towel and rest for 30 minutes at room temperature.

2. Once the dough has rested, add the oil or ghee and salt. Knead for a few minutes until it's well mixed and smooth. Cover and rest for 15-20 minutes.

3. Divide the dough into 30–40g balls and keep covered with a towel while you roll and cook each fulka.

4. Heat a dry non-stick flat pan over a high heat. Getting the pan hot is key to cooking correctly and getting that elusive puff, which comes from trapped steam that's trying to escape. To achieve this, the dough needs to cook and set on the outside before the interior cooks and releases steam.

5. Using a rolling pin and wooden board, roll each fulka out as thinly as you can, dipping or dusting with dry flour to prevent it sticking.

6. Hold the fulka up briefly to dust off any excess dry flour and place on the hot pan. Cook for 30 seconds, or until you see small bubbles appear on the surface, then flip over and cook for another 20–30 seconds. Flip over one final time. This is the magic flip where it should begin to puff up when gently pressed with a tea towel. Ideally, you'd pull the fulka off the pan and cook it directly over the flame at this stage with the help of tongs, but this requires a gas burner and some practice.

7. Garnish with a drizzle of ghee or butter and serve hot. You can make these ahead of time and keep them wrapped in a clean tea towel. Spread some fat on them before stacking to keep them soft. Any leftover dough can be kept refrigerated in an airtight container for up to two days. Allow it to come to room temperature before rolling and cooking.

Masala Theplas

Makes 10–12

*****

200g chapati flour, plus extra
for rolling

50g natural or Greek-style yoghurt

1 tsp white sesame seeds

½ tsp Kashmiri red chilli powder

½ tsp ground turmeric

2 tsp dried fenugreek leaves
(optional)

½ tsp carom seeds (optional)

¾ tsp salt

1 tbsp finely chopped fresh
fenugreek or coriander leaves

2 tsp neutral oil, plus extra
for cooking

These spiced flatbreads are a Gujarati staple. We have stacks in our freezer, courtesy of friends and family from India who never visit without a stash of them. They are delicious as a simple snack alongside a pickle, or served with a full meal.

The generous amount of oil used in cooking theplas ensures that they don't spoil easily and that they stay soft and supple. If, however, you're making them for immediate consumption, feel free to reduce the quantity of oil you use.

1. In a large mixing bowl, combine the flour, yoghurt, sesame seeds, chilli powder, turmeric, dried fenugreek, carom seeds, salt and chopped fresh herbs. Mix everything together thoroughly, then add the oil and mix well.

2. Gradually add 120–140ml water, little by little (you may not need it all), and knead the mixture into a soft, pliable dough. The dough should be smooth and not sticky. Cover and rest it for 20–30 minutes.

3. When ready to cook, divide the dough into approximately 30–40g portions. One at a time, roll each out thinly into a circle with a diameter of about 15cm, using a rolling pin and a little dry flour if you need it.

4. Heat a flat pan over a medium heat. Sprinkle over a few drops of oil and, once they shimmer, place a thepla on the pan. Cook for 30 seconds on the first side until you see it bubbling up, then flip and cook the other side for another 30 seconds while you brush the top with some oil. Increase the heat to medium-high and continue flipping and cooking for 15 seconds on each side, brushing the top with oil each time you flip. Each thepla will take 3–4 minutes and about ¾ teaspoon of oil to cook. (Any leftover dough can be kept refrigerated in an airtight container for up to two days. Allow it to come to room temperature before rolling and cooking.)

5. Once cooked, serve immediately or stack the theplas and keep them wrapped in a clean tea towel or foil parcel. Gujarati families, including ours, always have little stacks of foil-wrapped theplas in the freezer. They make great snacks, served alongside a nice pickle. They can be served warm or at room temperature.

Malabar Parotta

Makes 5–7

*****

1 egg

100ml whole milk

1 tsp sugar

1 tsp salt

300g plain flour, plus extra
   for dusting

3–4 tbsp neutral oil, for oiling
   and cooking

These coiled breads from Kerala are as much fun to eat as they are to make. If you haven't eaten one before, think of them as flattened croissants combining crisp golden wafer-thin layers on the outside with soft and stretchy bits of roti hidden within.

   Getting the crisp flaky layers right requires a bit of technique and practice, but I've simplified the process here to ensure you get it right from the very first time. *See overleaf for pictures of the technique.*

1. In a large mixing bowl, beat the egg and mix in the milk, sugar and salt. Gradually add the flour and stir well. Slowly drizzle in 2–3 tablespoons of water while kneading until the dough comes together. You might not need all the water; stop when the dough reaches the consistency of smooth playdough. It should feel soft and moist but not sticky. Transfer to a work surface and knead for a further 5 minutes. Cover with a clean tea towel or cling film and let it rest for 1 hour.

2. Divide the rested dough into 80–100g portions, shaping each into a ball, and place on a tray. Generously coat each ball with oil, cover the tray with cling film and leave to rest for 1 hour, or overnight in the fridge.

3. Roll out each dough ball on a well-oiled work surface into a thin disc, about 5mm thick. Leave to rest for 2–3 minutes. Begin stretching the first disc into a rectangle as far as you can without tearing. Use a rolling pin, if needed. Brush a thin layer of oil over the stretched dough and lightly sprinkle flour across it. Start pleating the dough from the end nearest to you to resemble a folded paper fan. Once fully pleated, coil the dough into a tight spiral, tucking the end underneath to keep it from unravelling. Repeat with the remaining discs, cover and leave to rest for a further 10 minutes.

4. When ready to cook, preheat a frying pan over a medium-high heat and roll one of the balls out to a 10–12cm disc. Add a splash of oil to the pan, followed by the first parotta, and cook for 1 minute. Flip the parotta and fry for a further minute, then continue to flip every 30 seconds until the parotta is golden and crisp. It should take 3–4 minutes in total. Repeat with the remaining parottas and either serve straight away or store in an airtight container until ready to eat. It is traditional to crush the parottas lightly just as they come off the pan, as this opens up all the layers to create an irresistible, fluffy, multi-layered bread that is perfect for mopping up curries.

Punjabi Parathas

Makes 8–9

*****

250g chapati flour

3 tbsp neutral oil or ghee

½ tsp salt

(see overleaf for variations)

This is one of those recipes that I hope you will come back to all the time. The basic dough recipe is so versatile – it works brilliantly on its own, and also as the wrapper for some delicious stuffed parathas. I've included some of my favourite variations (see overleaf); however, if you've not made parathas before, I recommend starting with this basic Punjabi paratha before trying the variations.

You can make the dough ahead of time or even cook the parathas and freeze them. At home, we keep a freezer drawer stocked with assorted rotis, parathas and other Indian breads. If you plan to freeze them, brush each paratha with ghee while it's still hot and wrap the stack tightly with foil or cling film. To reheat, you can warm them from frozen in a non-stick pan, or microwave them wrapped in a damp tea towel for 30 seconds to a minute.

1. In a mixing bowl, mix the flour with 100–120ml water just until a dough comes together, with no dry bits of flour remaining (you may not need all the water). There's no need to knead it further at this stage. Cover and let it rest for 15 minutes.

2. Add 1 tablespoon of oil or ghee and the salt to the dough. Knead for a minute until the fat is fully incorporated and you have a soft, smooth dough. The dough should not be sticky, but at the same time should not feel dry. Cover and rest it for 10–15 minutes, or for up to two nights in the fridge. If you rest it in the fridge, bring the dough to room temperature before continuing.

3. When ready to cook, divide the dough into approximately 50g portions. One at a time, roll each portion out thinly into a circle with a diameter of about 12–15cm, using a rolling pin and a little dry flour if you need to.

4. Brush the surface of the rolled-out dough with a little oil or ghee and fold it in half to form a semi-circle. Now brush the semi-circle with oil or ghee and fold it in half again to form a triangle. Roll out the triangle evenly, using dry flour as needed, into a larger 12–15cm triangle.

5. Heat a dry flat pan over a medium heat and place the paratha on it. Cook for a couple of minutes on the first side until you see it bubbling, then flip and cook the other side for a minute or two. Increase the heat to medium-high, add ½ teaspoon of oil or ghee to the pan, and flip the paratha again. Press it down gently with a spatula and keep flipping until the paratha is crisp and golden brown on the outside. Serve immediately.

Paratha Variations

Spiced Parathas

Spices such as carom seeds, fennel, cumin, coriander or even pomegranate seeds work wonderfully in parathas. Lightly toast a tablespoon of your favourite seeds and add it to the paratha dough at the same time as the ghee and salt. You can also mix ground spices such as turmeric or Kashmiri chilli powder directly into the dough without toasting them. Simply add these spices along with the ghee and salt, and mix thoroughly into the dough. The rest of the process remains the same.

Herby Parathas

Herbs such as fresh mint, fenugreek leaves (dried or fresh), or even dill add a unique flavour to parathas. Sprinkle a teaspoon of fresh herbs or ¼ teaspoon of dried herbs over the rolled-out circular dough brushed with ghee, before folding it into a semi-circle. Proceed as per the recipe.

Stuffed Parathas

An entire book could be written about the different ways in which a paratha can be stuffed. At its simplest, you can stuff parathas with mashed potatoes mixed with ginger, fresh coriander, toasted cumin, green chillies and chaat masala. Another delicious filling idea is simply grated cheese or a mix of different cheeses. If you want to start getting more adventurous, try grated radish, cauliflower, beetroot, leftover kheema matar or crumbled paneer. The options stretch as far as your imagination can go.

To stuff parathas, roll the dough into a 15–20cm circle, brush with ghee and place a small ball of filling in the centre. Pull the edges up to the centre and pinch them together to seal the stuffing inside. Carefully and evenly roll out the ball to a 12–15cm circle, ensuring that the dough does not split and the filling remains inside.

Puffy Fried Breads

I love the process of making fried bread. There is something magical about watching the unassuming flat discs of dough puff up as soon as they hit the hot oil. It's not something I do at home every day, but every now and then, it's a little indulgence we give in to. A treat for both the adults and kids.

   The most commonly eaten versions of puffy, balloon-like fried breads across India are puris (usually in Gujarat and Maharashtra in the west), luchis (mainly in West Bengal in the east) and bhaturas (in Delhi and other parts of North India). The main difference between a puri and a luchi is the use of wholewheat flour (or atta) in the former and white all-purpose flour (or maida) and sugar in the latter. I've included my recipe for puris overleaf, but you can swap the wholewheat flour for an equal amount of plain white flour and add ½ teaspoon sugar to the dough to make luchis. Bhaturas, on the other hand, are more complex, with the addition of yoghurt, potatoes and sometimes even yeast.

Puris

**Makes about 20 small
  puris**

*****

200g whole-wheat flour (ideally
  chapati flour)

25g fine semolina

½ tsp salt

1 tsp vegetable oil, plus extra
  to deep-fry

For me a freshly fried puri always brings back the fondest memories of childhood, sitting around my grandmother's table with my cousins, competing at who could eat the most puris. A game I wish my heart and gut would allow me to play today, with no consequence. We would devour them plain with steam billowing out, wrap them around our favourite Aloo Matar (page 58), or even dip them into sweets like Shrikhand (page 238) or freshly squeezed mango pulp. As weird as the last combinations might sound, try them and you won't be eating puris any other way.

1. Place all the ingredients in a mixing bowl along with 120–140ml warm water and knead briefly until you have a smooth, soft dough (you may not need all the water). This should take about 5–6 minutes. Shape the dough into a ball, rub a little oil over the surface, cover, and rest for 30 minutes.

2. When ready to cook the puris, divide the dough into 18–20g balls and roll them out into thin discs, approximately 9–10cm in diameter. If they stick to the rolling pin, apply a drop of oil to them rather than dry flour, which can burn in the hot oil while frying.

3. Heat the oil in a small wok, filling it no more than halfway, to 200°C.

4. Carefully lower the puris into the hot oil with a slotted spoon to avoid spills and splashes. Flip them over after about 10 seconds, as soon as they are fully puffed up, and continue to fry them for a further 20–30 seconds. Remove from the oil to briefly drain on kitchen paper and serve piping hot.

Bhaturas

Makes 12–14

*****

250g plain flour (ideally maida)

100g mashed potatoes, at room temperature

2 tbsp natural or Greek-style yoghurt

75g whole milk

1 tsp salt

1 tsp sugar

½ tsp baking powder

1 tbsp oil, plus extra to deep-fry

This north Indian fried bread is very different from puris and is traditionally eaten with Chole (see page 70), a chickpea curry. In Delhi, the chole bhatura holds cult status. Street vendors and restaurants famed for this dish often see long queues of eager diners waiting for a taste.

While traditional recipes vary, I personally like adding potatoes to the bhatura dough. I love what they bring to the bread in terms of both flavour and texture.

1. Place all the ingredients in a mixing bowl and mix well until you have a dough that's the consistency of smooth and soft playdough. It should feel soft and moist but not sticky. Transfer the dough to a work surface and knead for 5 minutes.

2. Shape the dough into a ball, rub a little oil over the surface, cover and rest for 2 hours at room temperature.

3. When ready to cook the bhaturas, divide the dough into 30–40g balls and roll them out into thin ovals, approximately 12–15cm wide. If they stick to the rolling pin, apply a drop of oil to them rather than dry flour, which can burn in the hot oil while frying.

4. Heat the oil in a small wok, filling it no more than halfway, to 170–180°C.

5. Carefully lower the bhaturas into the hot oil with a slotted spoon to avoid spills and splashes. Flip over after about 10–20 seconds, as soon as they are fully puffed up, then continue to fry them for a further 30–45 seconds until light brown and cooked through. Remove from the oil to briefly drain on kitchen paper.

6. Serve them piping hot, and be sure to watch the reaction of your diners when they poke holes in their bhaturas!

Stovetop Naans

Makes 10 small naans

*****

100g whole milk

2 tsp sugar

1 tsp salt

50g natural or Greek-style yoghurt

1 tbsp ghee or melted butter, plus
    more to garnish (optional)

300g self-raising flour

Naans require a tandoor, the famous north Indian clay oven, to be made properly. Anyone who tells you these can be made in an oven is simply selling you a recipe for a flatbread or pitta. The naan is brushed with water on one side, encouraging it to stick to the walls of the preheated tandoor when slapped on to it. This leads to its characteristic bubbly top and smooth bottom. Popping naan dough into an oven makes it puff up like a balloon rather than bubble up in its characteristic fashion. The only way I have found to mimic the tandoor effect is to cook this on a cast-iron or stainless-steel pan, heated over a gas stove. Non-stick pans don't work, as the naan won't (or shouldn't) stick to them. A further hack, if you don't have a gas burner, is to begin cooking the naans on the stove and finish them under the grill of your oven. I've set out details of both methods below.

1. In a large mixing bowl, combine the milk, sugar, salt, yoghurt and 1 tablespoon of ghee (or melted butter). Gradually add the flour and stir well, then slowly drizzle in 2–3 tablespoons of water while kneading until the dough comes together. You might not need all the water; stop when the dough reaches the consistency of smooth and soft playdough. It should feel soft and moist, but not sticky. Transfer the dough to a work surface and knead for a further 5 minutes, then cover it with a clean tea towel or cling film and let it rest for 1 hour.

2. After resting, divide the dough into 50–60g balls, keep them covered with cling film, and allow them to rest for 10–15 minutes.

3. Roll each rested dough ball on a lightly floured surface into a 5mm thick oval, about 12–15cm long by 10–12cm wide.

4. To cook the naans, heat a cast-iron pan over a medium-high heat until hot. One at a time, brush one side of a naan with some water, then carefully slap the wet side of the naan on to the pan. The naan should stick to the pan and begin to bubble after 30 seconds to 1 minute. After a minute, if cooking over a gas flame, carefully turn the pan over with the naan stuck to the pan, to hover a few centimetres above the direct flame. It should begin to char wonderfully. Move the pan around to ensure that it is evenly charred and cooked. After about a minute, turn the pan right way up again and remove the naan from the pan with a thin spatula or knife. If the naan is cooked through, it should peel off the pan easily. If it doesn't come off, continue cooking pan side down for another 20–30 seconds and

try again. If you don't have a gas stove, you can cook the top side of the naan on the highest shelf, under the grill of an oven set on maximum heat, for 1–2 minutes, until charred in spots. If it doesn't come off the pan easily after this time, return the pan to the stove and continue cooking pan side down for another 20–30 seconds, then try again.

5. Optionally brush the naans with melted butter or ghee, and serve immediately or wrap in foil or a clean tea towel to keep them warm.

Sindhi Kokis

Makes 4–5

*****

200g chapati flour

80g red onions, finely chopped

1 tsp coriander seeds

½ tsp cumin seeds

2 tsp finely chopped fresh
    coriander leaves

1 green chilli, finely chopped

½ tsp dried pomegranate seeds
    (optional)

¾ tsp salt

2 tsp neutral oil, plus extra
    for cooking

If you're new to Indian breads, this recipe is a great place to start. Kokis are wheat flatbreads, popular in the Sindhi community in India, remarkably easy and forgiving to make, yet delicious. They are perfect as a snack or side dish. The addition of chopped vegetables and spices to the dough imparts a wonderful flavour and a rich texture. Kokis are traditionally cooked over a medium heat while being frequently brushed with oil, giving them a distinctive flaky texture and biscuity exterior, with a soft and moist centre.

1. In a large mixing bowl, combine the flour, red onions, coriander seeds, cumin seeds, fresh coriander leaves, green chilli, dried pomegranate seeds (if using), salt and oil. Mix everything together thoroughly.

2. Gradually add 120–150ml warm water, little by little, and knead the mixture into a firm dough. You may not need all the water. The dough should be slightly stiffer than regular chapati dough. Cover and rest it for about 15–20 minutes.

3. Divide the dough into approximately 80–100g pieces. One at a time, roll each piece into a thick, round disc, about 12cm in diameter. Each koki should be thicker than a regular paratha, about 3–4mm thick.

4. Heat a flat pan over a medium heat. Sprinkle over a few drops of oil and once they shimmer, place a koki on the pan. Cook for 2 minutes. Flip the koki and cook the other side for another 2 minutes.

5. Drizzle some oil around the edges of the koki and brush some over the top. Continue to cook, flipping every 30–45 seconds, and brushing with oil each time, until both sides are golden brown and crisp. Each koki should take about 5–6 minutes to cook completely. When cooked, the koki should be crisp and spotted on the outside and soft within. Don't worry if they begin to break on occasion, they will still be delicious.

6. Kokis can be served hot or at room temperature, and make a great snack alongside a simple pickle or yoghurt. Alternatively, they can be served as part of a main meal.

Yellow Lentil Chillas

Makes 6–8

*****

150g yellow husked lentils
   (mung dal)

1 tbsp fine semolina

½ tsp ground turmeric

½ tsp cumin seeds

1 green chilli, finely chopped

1cm ginger, grated

a large pinch of asafoetida
   (optional)

½ tsp salt

3–4 tbsp neutral oil (or ghee or
   butter), to cook

Growing up, we used to have these chillas as a quick alternative to dosas, especially when my mum was short of time or hadn't soaked rice overnight for dosa batter. Nowadays, these lentil pancakes have earned a permanent spot in my kitchen, no longer just a substitute. They're incredibly easy to make, quick, healthy and wonderfully versatile crowd-pleasers. You can tweak the spices in the batter to your liking and enjoy them as a light breakfast with chutney and yoghurt, or stuff them with potatoes, paneer or minced meat and roll them up into a delicious wrap.

  If you have any leftover batter, it can be refrigerated for up to three days or frozen on the day it's made.

1. Wash the lentils until the water runs clear, then soak them for 3–4 hours.

2. Drain the soaked lentils and blend, adding 50–60ml of water until you have a batter the consistency of thin pancake batter.

3. Pour the batter into a large mixing bowl and add all the ingredients except the oil, mixing well. Cover and allow to rest for 15–20 minutes.

4. After resting, add 30–50ml of water, if required, to bring the batter back to a thin consistency.

5. Heat a large flat non-stick pan over a medium-high heat and add a few drops of oil. Once the oil shimmers, spread it evenly over the pan with a clean towel or kitchen paper.

6. Ladle some batter on to the pan, spreading it across the pan with the help of a spoon or the bottom of the ladle to form a 15–20cm circle, working as swiftly as possible. Don't worry about getting the chilla too thin, these are fairly thick traditionally.

7. Drizzle some oil all over the chilla and cook for 2–3 minutes. Then peel the chilla off the pan carefully and flip for 30 seconds. Flip back over, fold in half and serve immediately.

8. Wipe the pan and repeat the process to make more chillas, stirring the batter very well each time. Any remaining batter can be stored in an airtight container in the fridge for up to 3 days.

Sweets

Mango Ice-cream Sticks

Makes 8

*****

2 ripe Alphonso or Kesar mangoes,
  or 300g tinned mango pulp

300g double cream

sugar or preferred sweetener,
  to taste

400g white chocolate

2 tbsp coconut oil (optional)

I first began making these little ice-cream sticks at home as a healthier alternative to store-bought versions. Almost instantly they proved to be such a great success with all age groups that I had to start stocking boxes of them in my freezer for spontaneous visits from my sons' friends (and their parents). They are also particularly handy to serve at dinner parties where you don't have the energy to make dessert but refuse to outsource it.

For a wonderful twist on these, add the seeds of two cardamom pods and a pinch of saffron to the mango mix before setting them. Saffron and cardamom work beautifully together, and are a very popular combination in milky desserts in India.

You will need ice-lolly moulds for these. I use mini silicone moulds, but kulfi moulds or even small disposable plastic cups can work well.

1. If you're using fresh mangoes, start by peeling, chopping and blending them into a smooth pulp.

2. In a mixing bowl, combine the mango pulp and cream, then add sugar or sweetener, to taste (this may depend on how sweet your mangoes are). Whisk until the mixture is thick and fully combined. You can also use a mixer to blend it until it reaches a thick, milkshake-like consistency.

3. Spoon the mixture into ice-cream or lolly moulds and pop a wooden stick in. Cover and freeze overnight.

4. Once the ice-cream sticks have set, chop the white chocolate and combine with the coconut oil (if using) in a narrow microwaveable glass. Microwave on high for a minute or two, stopping and stirring every 20 seconds until the chocolate has fully melted. Let it cool slightly to avoid melting the ice cream when dipping.

5. Remove the ice-cream sticks from the moulds and very quickly dip them into the melted chocolate. Let any excess chocolate drip back into the glass and place the stick on a tray lined with baking parchment to set. Repeat to coat the other sticks. Once coated, they can be served immediately or returned to the freezer until ready to serve.

6. Any excess chocolate can be stored in a covered container in the fridge for up to a week. If it's cold where you are, you may need to reheat it before dipping the next batch of ice-cream sticks.

Carrot Halwa

Serves 4–6

*****

3 tbsp ghee

350g carrots, peeled and
    coarsely grated

300ml full-fat milk

100g condensed milk or
    granulated sugar

2 green cardamom pods,
    seeds only

a grating of nutmeg

a pinch of saffron, soaked in
    a tablespoon of warm milk
    (optional)

a pinch of salt

2 tbsp each of cashews, almonds
    and raisins

As kids, we'd wait patiently for winter when the sweetest red carrots were in season, and this irresistible Punjabi dessert was made in every home. It's arguably one of India's most popular desserts and a common item on Indian menus across the globe. I love a warm carrot halwa, and despite its decadence, I try to justify an extra helping by arguing that it's contributing to my five-a-day.

Over the years I've made this with every type of carrot. While I still get nostalgic about the deep red hues of gajar halwa on a cold wintery evening in Delhi, I've found that a purple carrot halwa on an autumn day in London can be equally magical. Use carrots of any colour you like, just make sure they are the best quality you can find, as they really are the star of the show here.

1. Warm 2 tablespoons of ghee in a saucepan over a medium heat and add the grated carrots. Stir-fry for 30 seconds, then add 300ml of water.

2. Bring to the boil, then reduce to a simmer and cook until most of the water has evaporated. Add the milk and condensed milk and continue cooking over a low heat, stirring every now and then, until you have the consistency you like, approximately 20 minutes. I like to stop when it resembles a thick custard. Remember that it will continue to thicken as it gets cooler.

3. Crush the cardamom seeds as best you can with a rolling pin or in a pestle and mortar, and scrape them into the halwa along with the nutmeg, saffron and its soaking milk (if using), and salt.

4. Fry the nuts in the remaining tablespoon of ghee until golden, then add the raisins and continue frying for 15 seconds. Pour over the halwa and stir through, just before serving. I enjoy this dessert both warm or chilled.

Indian Bread Pudding

Serves 4–6

*****

100g ghee, or melted butter, plus
   extra for greasing

12 slices of stale white bread,
   crusts removed

1 litre whole milk

1 x 397g tin of condensed milk

150g sugar, to taste

a pinch of saffron, soaked in
   2 tbsp milk

¼ tsp ground cardamom, or seeds
   from 2 pods, crushed

¼ tsp ground nutmeg (optional)

40g almonds, roughly chopped

40g raisins

This recipe takes inspiration from Hyderabad's shahi tukda, a dish typically made by frying bread in ghee and soaking it in a thick, rich rabdi, which is created by simmering full-fat milk for hours until it reduces to a fraction of its original volume. My version offers a relatively lighter, easier and quicker alternative to the classic, requiring a lot less tending to and allowing the oven to do all the heavy lifting.

1. Preheat your oven to 180°C fan. Grease a large baking dish with ghee or butter.

2. Cut the bread slices into triangles, spread all but 1 teaspoon of ghee over them, and arrange them in the prepared dish.

3. In a mixing bowl, whisk together the milk, condensed milk and sugar until the sugar has dissolved. Add the saffron with its soaking milk, cardamom and nutmeg (if using) and mix well.

4. Pour the milk mixture evenly over the bread pieces, making sure all the bread is soaked. Let the bread soak in the milk mixture for about 10–15 minutes.

5. Place the baking dish in the preheated oven and bake for 30–35 minutes, or until the top is golden brown and a toothpick inserted into the centre comes out clean.

6. Now heat the remaining ghee in a small pan over a medium heat and fry the almonds until golden. Turn the heat off and add the raisins, letting them cook in the residual heat for a minute, stirring constantly. Sprinkle this mix over the pudding and serve it warm or chilled.

Baked Caramel Yoghurt

Serves 4–6

*****

2 tbsp sugar

800g Greek-style yoghurt

1 x 397g tin of condensed milk

200ml full-fat milk

⅓ tsp ground green cardamom,
or seeds of 3 cardamom pods,
crushed (see page 238)

passionfruit pulp, or fresh fruit of
your choice, to serve (optional)

In the 1990s, Philadelphia-style cream cheese was hard to find in India, making it challenging to follow typical Western cheesecake recipes. As a result, the famous Bengali baked yoghurt dessert bhapa doi was often served as a substitute in our home. Mum would top it with freshly cut mangoes or strawberries for a delightful fruity twist. I love adding a dollop of fresh passionfruit pulp to it, for a delicious tang and crunch.

While traditional recipes don't include condensed milk, I find that using it adds a richer, creamier texture and prevents the yoghurt splitting.

1. Preheat your oven to 180°C fan. Place a deep baking dish or a roasting pan inside and fill it halfway with boiling water. This will create a water bath to bake the yoghurt in.

2. Put the sugar into a small pan set over a medium heat and allow it to melt and caramelize, swirling the pan occasionally but not stirring, until it turns a deep amber colour. Be careful not to burn it. Once ready, add 100ml of boiling water to the caramel, being very careful as it will be very hot and can splash and burn. Keep stirring until the caramel melts, then allow it to cool slightly.

3. In a mixing bowl, whisk together the caramel, yoghurt, condensed milk, milk and cardamom until smooth and well combined.

4. Pour the yoghurt mixture into a large baking dish, or individual ramekins or earthen bowls, and seal them tightly with tin foil.

5. Place the filled dish or dishes in the preheated water bath in the oven and bake for 40–45 minutes, or until the yoghurt is set but still slightly wobbly in the centre.

6. Remove the dish or dishes from the oven and allow to cool to room temperature. Refrigerate for at least 2 hours, or ideally overnight, until fully chilled and set.

7. Serve chilled, topped with passionfruit pulp or your favourite fresh fruit, if you like.

Kashmiri Phirni

Serves 4–6

*****

1 litre full-fat milk

1 x 397g tin of condensed milk

80g semolina

⅓ tsp ground green cardamom, or
   seeds from 3 cardamom pods,
   crushed (see page 238)

a pinch of saffron, soaked in
   2 tbsp milk

60g pistachios and almonds,
   thinly sliced

¼ tsp rose water (optional)

1 tbsp dried rose petals, to
   decorate (optional)

I find the intense sweetness and richness of many Indian desserts quite overwhelming. However, this pudding stands out, with its subtle, aromatic flavours that hit all the right notes. The rose water and saffron impart a delightful fragrance and a nuanced backdrop to the dish, while the crunchy nuts add a beautiful contrast in texture. I choose not to add any extra sugar, as the condensed milk and natural sweetness of the milk provide just the right amount. Some cooks make this dish with short-grain rice that has been soaked and crushed, but I prefer using coarse semolina for the ideal texture. If you opt for fine semolina, be sure to use a bit less, as it tends to absorb more liquid.

1. Mix together the milk and condensed milk in a heavy pan and bring to the boil. Reduce the heat to low and add the semolina, stirring constantly to avoid lumps. Cook the mixture over a low heat, stirring often, until the mixture thickens to the consistency of a rich custard, about 15–20 minutes. Remember, it will continue to thicken once it cools and the semolina absorbs more moisture, so avoid reducing it too much at this stage.

2. Add the cardamom and soaked saffron, and continue to cook for another 3 minutes.

3. Once the phirni reaches your desired consistency, turn off the heat. Stir in the sliced nuts and the rose water (if using). Mix well and pour the phirni into individual serving bowls or earthen pots. Allow it to cool to room temperature, then cover and refrigerate for at least 2 hours, or overnight.

4. Serve chilled, decorated with dried rose petals, if you like.

Easy Ladoos

Makes 15–20

*****

110g ghee

250g gram flour

¼ tsp ground cardamom

a pinch of saffron (optional)

50g mixed almonds and
   pistachios, toasted
   and roughly chopped

180–200g granulated sugar

Ladoos are one of the most iconic Indian sweets, right up there with gulab jamuns and jalebis. Picture an Indian halwai's shop – a stall overflowing with sweets of every shape, colour and size, all expertly crafted and generously laden with ghee. Ladoos often take centre stage, making them a popular choice for gifting during auspicious occasions or for offering to Hindu deities at temples. This version is one of the simplest, requiring just a handful of ingredients, and can be prepared in minutes.

1. Heat the ghee in a non-stick pan over a medium heat. Once fully melted, reduce the heat, then add the gram flour and cook, stirring constantly to combine it with the ghee and make sure it doesn't burn. Keep cooking for 30–35 minutes. It will resemble wet sand, but as you continue cooking and stirring the mixture, it will turn to a peanut butter consistency and smell beautifully nutty. Don't try to rush this process, or leave it unattended, as it can burn very easily. The slow roast is essential to the characteristic nutty flavour of the ladoos.

2. Take the pan off the heat, add the cardamom and saffron, mix well, then allow the mixture to cool until just warm to the touch.

3. Add the nuts and sugar and mix thoroughly, then roll the mixture into 4cm balls between your palms. Place on a plate and allow the ladoos to cool to room temperature.

4. You can serve these immediately, or store them in an airtight container for up to a week at room temperature.

Bengali Sandesh

Makes 8–10 pieces

*****

1 litre full-fat milk

60ml lemon or lime juice

75g powdered jaggery,
   or 50g granulated sugar

a pinch of salt

1 tsp ground cardamom

chopped nuts and saffron
   (optional)

Sandesh, a beloved Bengali dessert, is crafted from the velvety curds of split milk, called chenna. While the method of creating chenna is similar to that of making paneer, there's a subtle yet crucial difference – the tender curds aren't pressed, preserving their soft, delicate texture. This is what gives sandesh its irresistible, melt-in-the-mouth quality.

When I use white sugar instead of jaggery in sandesh, I like to add a hint of rose water. For this version, I skip the usual nuts and saffron, choosing instead to finish it with a delicate decoration of fresh rose petals.

1. Boil the milk over a medium heat, stirring constantly to prevent a skin forming on the surface or the milk sticking to the pan. Once it reaches the boil, let it simmer for 2 minutes.

2. Take the milk off the heat and pour in the lemon or lime juice. Stir gently and set aside for 3–4 minutes. The milk should split, with the whey turning a clear greenish colour. If it remains cloudy, add a bit more lemon juice and warm gently until it clears.

3. Once the milk has fully split, add a few ice cubes to stop the curds overcooking and to keep them soft.

4. Strain the mixture through a sieve lined with a clean tea towel or muslin cloth. Set aside the whey and wash the curds under running water to remove any residual sourness. Wrap the curds tightly in the cloth and hang it over a sieve for 30 minutes to drain any excess liquid.

5. Transfer the drained curds onto a large flat plate and knead with the palm of your hand until the mixture becomes smooth and creamy.

6. Add the jaggery, salt and cardamom to the kneaded curds and mix thoroughly.

7. Shape the mixture into small balls or logs, or use small moulds to create your desired shapes.

8. Decorate with chopped pistachios or almonds and saffron strands, if using.

Rice and Jaggery Payasam

Serves 4–6

*****

100g pudding rice

800ml full-fat milk

a pinch of salt

3–4 green cardamom pods

80–100g jaggery, to your taste

200ml coconut milk

1 tbsp coconut oil

2 tbsp cashews, roughly chopped

1 tbsp raisins

Milky rice desserts are beloved in India. Kheers and phirnis in the north, and pongals and payasams in the south – all are delicious versions of Indian 'rice pudding'. This recipe is traditionally made with a variety of short-grain rice from Kerala, but I find pudding rice gives it a creamier texture and is a lot easier to find in the West.

Jaggery can be substituted with raw palm sugar, coconut sugar, dark brown sugar, muscovado sugar or even maple syrup. Each of these will have a different level of sweetness, so adjust to your taste.

1. Put the rice, along with the whole milk, 200ml of water and the salt, into a deep pan set over a medium-high heat. Once it comes to the boil, reduce the heat to low and simmer until the rice is fully cooked and the milk has reduced by two-thirds, about 15–20 minutes.

2. Remove the seeds from the cardamom pods and crush them using a pestle and mortar or a rolling pin. Add the crushed seeds to the rice mixture, along with the jaggery and coconut milk. Continue to simmer until the pudding reaches a creamy consistency, about 8–10 minutes. You can prepare this rice pudding in advance and either reheat it before serving or enjoy it cold. If reheating, you might need to add a splash of milk to adjust the consistency, as it tends to thicken over time.

3. Just before serving, heat the coconut oil in a small pan and fry the cashews for about 30 seconds, or until they turn a shade darker. Add the raisins and fry for another 10 seconds. Either pour this mixture into the pudding and stir well, or use to decorate the top of each individual serving.

Cashew Barfi

Makes 18–20 pieces

*****

250g cashew nuts

110g granulated or caster sugar

¼ tsp ground cardamom

a pinch of saffron (optional)

1 tbsp ghee, plus (optional) extra
  for greasing

Celebrations and festivals in India wouldn't be complete without barfis, ladoos and the hundreds of other traditional sweets sold by halwais (Indian confectioners) across the country. Among all these sweets, my favourite was always kaju katli, also known as cashew barfi. Typically covered in edible silver and cut into diamond shapes, no festive dessert spread was complete without it. These treats were almost always purchased from sweet shops, and it wasn't until I was living in the UK and craving them that I realized how easy they were to make at home. Occasionally, I even go the extra mile and source edible silver or gold leaf to cover them. While this only adds a visual aesthetic, it indulges my sense of nostalgia.

1. Grind the cashew nuts to a very fine powder. A few pulses in a blender or food processor should do the trick. Avoid leaving the grinder running for longer than a few seconds, though, as this could cause the cashews to split and turn to cashew butter. Sift the powder to remove any larger pieces, and grind them again, until everything is fine.

2. Put the sugar and 50ml of water into a non-stick pan over a medium heat and stir until the sugar has dissolved completely.

3. Reduce the heat and add the ground cashews to the sugar syrup. Stir constantly to avoid lumps. Continue cooking and stirring the mixture for 5–7 minutes, until it starts to leave the sides of the pan.

4. Add the cardamom, saffron (if using) and ghee to the mixture and stir well. Continue cooking until the mixture thickens and forms a dough-like consistency. Be careful not to overcook it, as this can make the barfi hard. You are aiming for a soft, pliable texture, like playdough.

5. Transfer the cashew mixture onto a sheet of baking parchment greased with ghee or a piece of cling film. Place another sheet of greased parchment or cling film over it and roll it out to your desired thickness, using a rolling pin or a bottle laid on its side.

6. Allow the mixture to cool and set completely, about 2–3 hours at room temperature. Once cooled, cut into squares or diamond shapes and store in an airtight container for up to a week.

GOOD

to

KNOW

THE INDIAN PANTRY

When I first moved to the UK in the early 2000s, a significant portion of my baggage allowance was dedicated to spices and ingredients from Mumbai. Back then, many items were simply unavailable, and those that were fell far short of the quality I was used to back home. Fast forward to today, and things have changed dramatically. Now, there are many exceptional spices and blends available in most Western supermarkets and grocery stores.

The recipes in this book are designed with accessibility in mind. Most of the fresh and dry ingredients should be readily available at large supermarkets, online or occasionally at an Asian grocer. I always recommend buying spices in bulk – that is, in the larger packets that can be found in Asian grocers or larger supermarkets rather than the small glass jars – as they're more cost-effective that way. Always choose the best quality you can find.

*****

Once you have your spices, I encourage you to truly get to know them. Don't use them simply because the recipe says so – explore how they impact the dish and how they might complement or enhance other things you cook. For instance, adaptable recipes like Masala Beans (page 84) or Achari Traybake (page 137) are perfect for experimentation and making the most of your favourite spices, letting you create something uniquely your own.

Cupboard Ingredients

OILS AND FATS

Where a recipe simply says 'oil' it refers to a neutral oil that won't add any additional flavours to the dish, in which case I recommend a good-quality light rapeseed, groundnut, vegetable or sunflower oil. Do not use olive oil. Where a recipe benefits from a specific oil, it will be specified by name.

Coconut Oil

Coconut oil is a staple in south Indian cooking, enhancing both sweet and savoury dishes. While available in refined and virgin varieties, I prefer virgin coconut oil for its distinct flavour and aroma. Quality virgin coconut oil solidifies when cool; simply warm the jar or microwave it briefly to return it to liquid form.

Mustard Oil

This pungent and distinctive oil is a key ingredient in many Indian dishes, particularly in East and North India. Its bold flavour adds an inimitable depth to curries and pickles. It can be used raw for a sharp, robust taste, or heated until it begins to smoke then cooled before use to achieve a milder flavour.

Ghee

Ghee is similar to clarified butter but boasts a rich, nutty flavour that defines many Indian dishes. Revered for its Ayurvedic benefits, it is widely used in both savoury and sweet recipes, particularly in North and West India. While ghee is readily available in most supermarkets today, it's very easy to make at home (see page 94) with just a little time and good-quality butter. It can be substituted with oil, if preferred.

*****

SPICES

If you're likely to use ground spices less frequently, I think it's better to buy whole spices and grind them fresh, when needed. When substituting ground spices for whole, use less (about ¾ teaspoon ground for every 1 teaspoon of whole), as ground spices are more potent. Always add ground spices later in the cooking process to prevent burning and avoid frying them in oil for more than a few seconds.

Aamchur

Aamchur is a powder made from dried unripe green mangoes. It has a fruity, sour flavour that adds freshness and tang to dishes like chutneys, marinades and chaats. It's usually added as a finishing spice towards the end of the cooking process. Substitute lemon or lime juice, tamarind or fruity vinegar if you can't find it.

Asafoetida

Asafoetida, or hing, has a strong, pungent aroma similar to garlic powder and is a staple in Indian cooking. Widely available in supermarkets, it is sold as a powder or granules. Rich in sulphur compounds, it mimics the smell of eggs and meat, adding remarkable depth of flavour to dishes even in tiny amounts. A small tub of this magic ingredient can last months.

Black Salt

Black salt, or kala namak, is a sulfuric, pungent, mineral-rich salt, commonly used in chaats, chutneys, raitas and spice blends, such as Chaat Masala (page 266). The overpowering smell can be unpleasant at first, but once added to dishes it blends in beautifully and gives them a distinctive flavour that's hard to mimic.

Substitute with chaat masala, Himalayan salt or your regular salt if you can't find it.

Cardamom

Fragrant green cardamom is widely used in Indian desserts, teas and savoury dishes. Its small pods contain intensely flavoured tiny black seeds. For desserts, I prefer grinding the seeds, while for savoury dishes, I simply bruise the pods and add them whole to preserve the delicate aroma of the seeds. The pods can be removed before serving if required.

The larger black cardamom pods have a bold, smoky flavour and are key ingredients in some biryanis and North Indian curries. Unlike green cardamom, they are rarely used in desserts.

Chilli

Dried chillies when mentioned in this book refer to red Kashmiri or Bydagi chillies, which are worth buying in bulk as they retain their flavour for months.

When chilli powder is required, opt for Kashmiri red chilli powder, known for its vibrant colour and mild flavour. If unavailable, unsmoked paprika can be used, although the colour and flavour of the dish will differ slightly.

Cinnamon

Whole cinnamon, native to Sri Lanka, is sold as delicate sticks with a subtle flavour. Cassia, commonly used in India, is a darker, harder bark with a much more intense flavour. If using cassia where a recipe calls for cinnamon, reduce the quantity specified in the recipe to avoid overpowering the dish.

Cumin, Coriander and Fennel (seeds and ground)

These spices are used extensively in both whole (seed) and powdered forms across many recipes. If you cook Indian food regularly, it's worth keeping both on hand. However, if you're likely to use them less frequently, it's better to buy them whole and grind them fresh with a pestle and mortar or spice grinder, when needed (see note, above left).

Curry Leaves

Fresh curry leaves have a distinctive herbal flavour. They're available at most Asian grocers, and if they're hard to find locally, it's worth buying in bulk when you can. Freeze any extras in an airtight bag – they may turn black but will retain their flavour. Dried curry leaves, on the other hand, lack the vibrant taste of fresh or frozen ones, so I generally avoid them.

Fenugreek Seeds and Leaves

The versatile fenugreek plant is essential to a lot of Indian cooking. Its dried yellow seeds are intensely bitter when eaten by themselves, but when fried gently release a distinctive aroma that is vital to a lot of South and West Indian cooking.

Fresh fenugreek leaves, commonly used in North and West India, are trickier to find outside specialist Asian stores. However, dried fenugreek leaves (kasoori methi) are widely available and add that signature flavour to many popular North Indian dishes, such as Chicken Makhani (page 144), Black Dal (page 72) and a number of kebabs and tikkas.

Mustard Seeds

Unless otherwise specified, I use black or brown mustard seeds instead of yellow ones and prefer the former for their stronger flavour. However, yellow mustard seeds can be used as a substitute if you can't find the others.

Turmeric

Unless mentioned otherwise, my recipes use ground turmeric. Turmeric is very commonly used in Indian cooking and highly valued for its vibrant colour, rich flavour and health benefits. Always buy high-quality turmeric, as cheaper varieties are often adulterated with added colours or impurities. Add turmeric early in the cooking process to soften its robust flavour and ensure it evenly colours the dish. Be cautious when handling, as even small amounts can stain nails, fingertips, clothes and surfaces. Use dry hands and clean any spills immediately with a dry cloth.

MSG

Without wanting to stir up a hornet's nest, I briefly want to discuss MSG (monosodium glutamate). You'd struggle to eat Chinese-style food across India (which is hugely popular) without coming across this ingredient in some form or other – it's commonly referred to as Ajinomoto, after the brand that made it famous. Having read a fair amount on the subject, there seems to be little confirmed evidence about its harm, unless of course you're allergic to it and have a reaction. There are cultures across Asia where MSG is used freely in a lot of the street food, with no real damage caused when it's consumed occasionally. Personally, I add a pinch of it when cooking Indo-Chinese dishes, as it enhances all the other flavours and brings them closer to the form I remember eating on the streets of Mumbai. If you're open to it, go ahead and sprinkle a bit into Chilli Paneer (page 99) or Kung Pao Potatoes (page 57).

*****

COCONUT

Coconut Milk

I usually use good-quality tinned Thai coconut milk. Unlike fresh coconut milk, tinned contains stabilizers that prevents it splitting when heated. If using freshly squeezed coconut milk, avoid boiling it and only add it towards the end and cook it very briefly.

Grated Coconut

Asian stores usually stock fresh or frozen grated coconut, that can be stored in the freezer for up to six months. If you can't find this, soak desiccated coconut in equal parts of hot water for 10 minutes, then squeeze out the water and use the coconut.

*****

DRIED PULSES

Lentils

It's essential to identify lentils correctly, because while two might look similar, their flavours when cooked can be very different. I've listed the Indian names of the different lentils below, as most large Asian stores tend to stock Indian brands that label packages with these names.

Chana Dal : Raw Bengal Gram or Split Chickpea Lentils
Masoor Dal : Red Lentils
Moong Dal / Mung Dal : Split Green Gram or Yellow Lentils
Tuvar Dal / Toovar Dal / Arhar Dal : Yellow Split Pigeon Pea Lentils
Urid Dal : Black Lentils

Beans and Chickpeas

For the best results I use soaked and boiled dried beans and chickpeas, but tinned ones can work well when in a hurry – just boil them in some water briefly to soften, as they're often too firm straight out the tin. When cooking dried beans and chickpeas, adding a pinch of bicarbonate of soda helps speed up the process, and a pressure cooker is ideal for cutting down cooking time.

*****

JAGGERY

Jaggery, also known as gur, is an unrefined natural sweetener made from sugarcane juice or palm sap. It has a rich, complex, caramel-like flavour. It comes in solid blocks, chunks or powdered form and can be grated, sprinkled or melted with water before using. It can be substituted for Thai palm sugar, molasses, golden syrup, dark brown sugar or regular granulated sugar, but quantities will need to be adjusted to your personal preference.

*****

RICE

The recipes in this book have been tested with basmati rice, the most popular and widely available type of Indian rice. However, India is home to hundreds of rice varieties, many of which are more nutritious and flavourful than basmati. If you can get hold of these, they are well worth trying. Different varieties, qualities and ages of rice may require slight adjustments to cooking times and liquid quantities.

*****

FLOURS

Chapati and Maida Flour

Chapati flour, or atta, is a finely milled whole-wheat flour, softer and smoother than the coarser wholemeal flour common in Western supermarkets. It's ideal for making soft rotis and flatbreads and is now widely available at most large supermarkets. If you can't find any, mix equal parts plain and wholemeal flour, grind as finely as possible in a blender, and sift to remove any large husks.

Maida is a finely milled refined flour used in India for baking and breads. For authentic results, use maida when specified in a recipe, although plain flour works as a substitute.

Gram Flour

Gram flour, or besan, is a very versatile gluten-free flour made from dried chickpeas, frequently used in Indian breads, sweets, curries and batters. A very handy ingredient in the Indian kitchen, I highly recommend getting yourself a bag of this. If, however, you are unable to find some, it can be substituted with plain flour, cornmeal, oat flour, ground almonds or coconut flour, depending on the recipe.

Semolina

Semolina, often referred to as rawa in India, is a coarse flour made from durum wheat. It's coarser than the popular Italian variety used for pasta making and is often roasted slightly for a nuttier flavour.

Fresh Ingredients

VEG

Aubergine

Aubergine, also known as brinjal in India, is a staple in wet and dry curries. When selecting aubergines, look for firm, shiny ones without blemishes. Any variety can be used, as long as you match the specified weight. Salting the cut pieces for a few minutes before wiping them dry helps reduce the amount of oil absorbed and ensures even cooking.

Chillies

Chillies, both fresh and dried, are essential in many of the recipes in this book. While often associated solely with heat, their flavour is just as, if not more, important than their heat or colour.

For recipes calling for fresh green chillies, look for pusa jwala, finger or rocket chillies. Thai green chillies can be used as a substitute, but use these sparingly as they are typically much hotter.

For dried chillies and chilli powder, see page 255.

Garlic and Ginger

Preparing ginger and garlic in advance can save a lot of time when cooking Indian dishes. For young ginger, leave the skin on and chop, grate or blend with water or oil. Peel and prepare garlic in the same way. Store in the fridge for 2–3 weeks or freeze for up to three months. Minced, grated or paste forms can be used interchangeably, but remember pastes tend to burn more easily. Avoid store-bought versions, as preservatives and vinegar can affect their flavour.

See also Flavour Hacks (page 12).

Onions

Indian onions (often called Bombay onions), with their light purple skin and pink flesh, are sweeter and more pungent than yellow or white onions. Red onions or banana shallots are the closest substitutes, while brown or yellow onions can work too, but won't provide the same intensity.

See also Flavour Hacks (page 12).

Potatoes

Maris Piper or Red Desiree potatoes are excellent all-rounders for frying, boiling or mashing. If a recipe simply calls for potatoes without specifying a type, use one of these varieties for the best results.

Tomatoes

Tomatoes in India are typically tarter and less sweet than those in the West, with tinned varieties being even sweeter due to their concentration. When cooking, choose soft, ripe tomatoes on the vine when possible. If ripe tomatoes aren't available, opt for tinned over unripe ones, but adjust the level of acid or sugar in the recipe accordingly.

Tamarind

Ready-made tamarind paste is widely available at Asian grocers, but strengths can vary by brand. Always taste a new brand before using and start with less than the recipe suggests, adjusting to your preference. Avoid pastes that taste artificial or overly sweet.

If using dried tamarind blocks to make your own paste, mix about 75g of the tamarind block with 250ml of boiling water, let it sit until cool enough to handle, then massage the pulp to dissolve it. Strain to remove seeds and fibres, extracting as much pulp as possible. Store the pulp in a jar in the fridge for up to a week.

Whatever type of tamarind you use, adjust the sourness to your personal preference, adding more towards the end of cooking, if needed. If tamarind isn't available, you can substitute it with lemon or lime juice, or vinegar.

*****

FISH

Popular Indian fish, such as pomfret, rohu, hilsa, bangra and pearlspot are now increasingly available frozen at South Asian grocers and fishmongers in larger cities. However, I've tried to suggest more readily available, sustainable and locally sourced fish in my recipes. If these aren't accessible, a quick online search can help you find suitable substitutes based on what's available in your region.

*****

MEAT

In India, meat is typically bought fresh from the butcher, with cuts differing from those in the West. While supermarket meat works well, here are a few tips to consider:

Mutton vs Lamb: Indian recipes traditionally call for mutton, which confusingly refers to goat meat. It has a leaner profile and a gamier flavour than lamb. The recipes in this book use lamb, but you can substitute goat, if available. Keep in mind that goat may require longer cooking, depending on the cut and age of the animal.

Stewing Cuts: For curries and slow-cooked dishes, choose bone-in cuts or stewing pieces, as they add depth and richness to the gravy. Indian recipes typically don't use pre-made stocks, as the bone-in cuts used naturally create a stock while simmering.

Chicken: Unless specified, always use skinless chicken, as the skin isn't commonly used in Indian cooking. Bone-in chicken is ideal for curries, as it enhances the flavour of the gravy and keeps the meat tender.

*****

DAIRY

Yoghurt
I have tested the recipes in this book using Greek yoghurt, unless specified otherwise. You can use natural yoghurt or even homemade yoghurt instead, but may need to adjust liquid quantities, as these are often thinner than Greek yoghurt. For those interested in making their own yoghurt, see page 95.

Paneer
Although ubiquitous across all Indian menus today, this cheese originated in northern India. It is considered a vital source of protein and calcium for vegetarians. It's fairly easy to find good-quality ready-made paneer in the cheese section of supermarkets, but if you'd like to make some at home, see page 93.

*****

KITCHEN NOTES

~~~~~~

Hobs and Ovens

I tested the recipes in this book on a gas hob, so if you're using induction or electric, you may need to adjust the cooking times slightly. The recipes are a helpful guide, but trust your senses – notice if the onions smell sweet and caramelized or if the sauce is boiling too rapidly and risks burning.

Oven temperatures refer to a domestic fan-assisted convection oven. An air fryer can often be used instead; simply lower the temperature, turn the food more frequently and reduce the cooking time.

Heavy Pan

Although a bit harder to handle, heavy cast-iron pans are excellent for their consistent heat distribution and retention, making them ideal for curries that require browning onions or meat. They're also great for slow-cooking curries and lentils, and the oven-safe pans are perfect for dishes that start on the hob and finish in the oven.

Karahi

A karahi, or kadhai, is a commonly used Indian cooking vessel, similar to a wok but thicker and heavier. It's typically made from copper, bronze, stainless steel or aluminium, and is widely used in Indian kitchens for stir-frying, deep-frying and simmering. The round bottom of a karahi is particularly useful for reducing the amount of oil used to stir-fry or deep-fry, but a heavy saucepan or cast-iron pan is a perfectly good substitute.

Spice Grinder or Pestle and Mortar

A small, inexpensive electric coffee grinder or a heavy pestle and mortar are both very useful for grinding small batches of spices.

Rolling Pin

An Indian rolling pin is slimmer and more dexterous than its chunkier Western counterpart, making it ideal for rolling out delicate fulkas, parathas and puris. Its characteristic tapered ends allow for easy rolling with minimal pressure. While not absolutely essential, it's a very useful and cheap addition to your kitchen – especially if, like me, you become obsessed with making Indian breads!

Deep-frying

At home, I use a medium-sized, round-bottomed, stainless-steel wok for deep-frying. It conducts heat well, and the round bottom helps me use less oil. Avoid overcrowding the pan and fry in batches to keep the temperature steady.

An air fryer can be a substitute, when specified, but some dishes require deep-frying. When done at the correct temperature, a deep-fried item will absorb less oil than one improperly shallow-fried, making it an excellent cooking method when used sparingly.

Salt and Seasoning

The salt quantities in my recipes are guidelines, not exact measures. I have used fine sea salt when testing recipes, so adjust based on your salt type and taste preferences. Start with less salt and add more during the final minutes of cooking. Unlike Western dishes, Indian food is seasoned while cooking to ensure the salt dissolves and blends evenly – never at the table. If a dish is too salty, you can often fix it by adding fat (such as coconut milk, oil, yoghurt or butter), a sweet or acidic ingredient (such as lime juice or sugar), or bulk starches (such as potatoes or cooked rice) to balance the flavours.

SPICE BLENDS

Garam masala is often thought of as the go-to spice mix for all Indian curries. Sadly, this belief is as much of a fallacy as using the term 'curry' as a catch-all for anything that finds its roots in the Indian subcontinent. Equally, there is no such thing as 'curry powder' in India.

In India we use various blends of spices; some are specific to a particular dish – pav bhaji masala, rasam masala, chana masala, etc. – while others are used across a variety of dishes – chaat masala, kebab masala, garam masala, etc. Store-bought versions of these often do the trick, and my larder at home is filled with brands I like. However, the flavour of the same

spice mix can differ vastly from brand to brand, as it does from home to home. So finding a brand you like can take some trial and error.

I've shared some basic recipes for blends we come back to time and again in this book. Since you're taking the trouble to make these at home instead of buying them, I encourage you to taste them as you go, tweak them to your liking and explore using them in your day-to-day cooking too. Nothing is too experimental – I know friends from India who've travelled round Italy with chaat masala and sprinkled it over pasta and pizza.

A Brief History of the Ubiquitous Madras Curry Powder

Madras curry powder dates to the 18th century but became popular during the British rule of India from the mid-19th century. When British expats returned home, they sought to replicate the flavours they had grown to love in India. Indian chefs would use freshly ground spices, but this proved to be impractical back home. The efficient solution was to create generic spice blends that could simply be sprinkled into dishes to replicate some of the flavours. It's said there were different blends representing different regional cuisines of India, but in the end the Madras blend (named after the south Indian port city, now known as Chennai) was the only one that remained.

Some say because it was the spiciest of the lot, but it's more likely because Madras was a key port that saw the most comings and goings.

Despite criticism from some Indian cooks, the spice blend is the most popular and commonly found 'Indian' ingredient across stores in the UK, and has found itself part of the cuisines of South Africa, the Caribbean and other present-day and former British colonies. My personal view is to embrace this omnipresent ingredient rather than criticize it for its origins. It might not have a place in authentic Indian cookery, but at least it introduces newcomers to flavours that wouldn't otherwise have made it into their kitchens.

All-purpose Chaat Masala

Makes about 250g
*****

50g cumin seeds

50g coriander seeds

15g fennel seeds

10g carom seeds

10–15 fresh mint leaves

10g black peppercorns

50g dried mango powder
 (aamchur, see page 255)

25g black salt

½ tsp Kashmiri red chilli powder

½ tsp ground ginger

15g salt

Unlike other spice blends, chaat masala is used as a finishing spice to sprinkle over dishes, rather than one that's added during the cooking process. It's one of my favourite things, and you're never more than an arm's length away from this wonderful tangy spice mix when having a meal in our home. Although intended to be sprinkled over streetside chaat dishes, this spice has a magical way of bringing almost anything to life, with its distinctive balance of heat and tang. It's truly addictive and so versatile – if you haven't tasted it yet, your life won't be the same once you have.

1. Begin by roasting the cumin, coriander, fennel and carom seeds in a dry pan set over a medium heat. Keep shaking the pan, and cook until the spices begin to smell aromatic and turn a slightly darker brown. Be careful not to over-roast or burn them.

2. Chop the mint leaves finely and add them to the hot spices in the pan. Give everything a good stir and continue to cook the mix on the lowest heat to dry the leaves completely, then take off the heat.

3. Allow the ingredients in the pan to cool completely, then combine with the remaining ingredients and grind it all to a fine powder. Pass through a fine-mesh sieve and store in an airtight container for up to 3 months.

Uses:
This tangy spice mix is best sprinkled over dishes just before serving, to give them an extra layer of zing.

In this book, see:
Potato Chaat (page 20)

Bombay Sandwich (page 27)

Potato Tuk (page 28)

Hara Kebabs (page 35)

Tandoori-style Roast Cauliflower (page 64)

Paneer Shashlik (page 100)

Salmon Tikka (page 106)

Reshmi Chicken Tikka (page 126)

Proper Butter Chicken (page 129)

Seekh Kebabs (page 130)

Raita (page 173)

Masala Papad (page 174)

Kachumber (page 176)

Lachcha Onions (page 179)

Simple Green Chutney (page 186)

Use on chaats; over eggs; on yoghurt; on grilled meats and kebabs; over cut fruit and vegetables; on crisps and nuts; mixed with melted butter and poured over popcorn or fresh corn; in a salad dressing; in drinks, such as lassis and Indian lemonade.

Basic Garam Masala

Makes 200g

*****

30g cumin seeds

100g coriander seeds

25g black peppercorns

5cm cassia bark (or cinnamon stick)

15g black cardamom pods

15g green cardamom pods

10g cloves

1 star anise

2 bay leaves

¼ nutmeg, grated

Garam masala translates literally as 'warm spice'. In India the term is used interchangeably to refer to whole spices such as cinnamon, cloves, cardamom, etc. or a blend of these, used to sprinkle into dishes towards the end. Unlike chaat masala, though, I don't like to sprinkle this over finished dishes, as it benefits from a few minutes of cooking. However, cook it for too long and the wonderful aromas of the spices will vanish. So sprinkle, stir, cook for a few minutes and serve.

1. Roast all but the nutmeg in a dry pan set over a medium heat. Keep shaking the pan and cook until the cumin and coriander begin to smell aromatic and turn a slightly darker brown. Be careful not to over-roast or burn them.

2. Take the pan off the heat and allow everything to cool completely. Now add the nutmeg and grind everything to a fine powder. Pass through a fine-mesh sieve and store in an airtight container for up to 3 months.

Uses:
This powerful, warming spice blend provides a boost of flavour to dishes. It's a great all-purpose spice mix to lift any dish, but particularly good for North and West Indian dishes.

In this book, see:
Hara Kebabs (page 35)
Burnt Aubergine Bharta (page 44)
Okra Yoghurt Curry (page 48)
Tandoori-style Whole Roast Cauliflower
  (page 64)
Chole (page 70)
Punjabi Rajma (page 76)
Dhaba Dal Fry (page 79)
Ros Omelette (page 88)

Paneer Shashlik (page 100)
Salmon Tikka (page 106)
Reshmi Chicken Tikka (page 126)
Proper Butter Chicken (page 129)
Seekh Kebabs (page 130)
Badami Chicken (page 143)
Chicken Makhani (page 144)
Kheema Matar (page 147)
BBQ Lamb Chop Curry (page 148)
Parsi Sali Boti (page 150)
Bihari One-Pot Meat Curry (page 155)
Kerala Beef Ishtew (page 158)

Use in baked beans; over hummus; in salad dressings; in marinades for grilled meat and veg; in bread; on roast vegetables; in soups and stews; in pasta; over tacos.

Biryani Masala

Makes about 150g

*****

50g coriander seeds

20g cumin seeds

25g fennel seeds

10g black peppercorns

5–6 cloves

4–5 green cardamom pods

2 black cardamom pods

5cm cassia bark
  (or cinnamon stick)

2–3 bay leaves

2 dried red chillies, seeds removed

10g Kashmiri red chilli powder

¼ nutmeg, grated

1 tsp ground turmeric

The biryani masala forms the bedrock of a biryani. And like the contentious topic of which biryani is best (see page 202 for more on the debate), choosing the perfect biryani masala isn't easy. Different regions use different spice blends and techniques. My go-to biryani masala is based on a Hyderabadi recipe, with some personal adaptations. More than any other spice mix, I strongly encourage you to make this your own. Don't be afraid of the long list of ingredients, adapt it as per your taste and store-cupboard.

1. Roast the coriander, cumin and fennel seeds in a dry pan set over a medium heat. Keep shaking the pan, and cook until the seeds begin to smell aromatic and turn a slightly darker brown. Be careful not to over-roast or burn them.

2. Take the pan off the heat and allow everything to cool completely. Now add the remaining ingredients and grind everything to a fine powder. Pass through a fine-mesh sieve and store in an airtight container for up to 3 months.

Uses:
This spice blend is the secret to a good biryani. If you make more than you need, it can also be used instead of garam masala.

In this book, see:
Easy Chicken Biryani (page 202)

Use sprinkled into soups; on roasts; in pilaus; in curries; to pep up fried rice.

How to Cook Perfect Rice

Cooking rice intuitively is a skill that many Indian mothers make look effortless. However, it requires a lot of practice and can be quite challenging. Overcooked rice can ruin an entire meal, so sometimes it's best to follow a formulaic approach rather than relying on instinct. Here's my formula for perfect basmati rice.

Washing basmati rice thoroughly to remove excess starch is crucial. While it's nearly impossible to get the water to run completely clear, aim for at least four or five changes of fresh cold water in a large bowl. Additionally, soaking the rice in cold water before cooking is essential. A 20-minute soak is optimal for achieving long, fluffy grains. Be cautious of soaking for much longer, as it can result in mushy rice when cooked.

This recipe works brilliantly with basmati rice. Different varieties of rice can absorb varying amounts of water, so if you're using a different variety, you may need to adjust the quantity of water. A dash of lime or lemon juice is a great trick to keep the rice sparkly white as it cooks.

Serves 4

*****

200g basmati rice
½ tsp salt (optional)
1 tsp rapeseed oil
15 drops of lemon or lime juice
a little ghee, to serve

1. Place the rice in a bowl and wash with several rounds of cold water, gently swirling it with your hands until the water runs somewhat clear.

2. Once washed, cover with fresh water and leave to soak for 20–30 minutes.

3. Drain the rice and place in a deep pan. Add 350ml of cold water, salt, oil and lemon or lime juice. Bring to the boil over a high heat and cook until the water level drops to the level of the rice, about 3 minutes.

4. Reduce the heat to low, cover the pan with a tight-fitting lid or foil and continue to cook for 15–20 minutes.

5. Turn off the heat and let the rice rest for 5 minutes, then remove the lid and gently fluff it up with a fork.

6. Dollop some ghee on top and serve immediately.

QUICK & EASY

Made in under 30 minutes of active cooking

~~~~~~~~

One of my goals in selecting the recipes for this book was to challenge the idea that all Indian food demands hours of effort and a long list of ingredients. A simple weekday meal can consist of a vegetable, lentil dish and rice, all put together in less than an hour. Some nights, my wife and I find nothing more comforting than a bowl of rajma with plain boiled rice, occasionally accompanied by a roasted papad and fresh green chillies. If you're after a really quick meal or snack, the recipes listed here involve less preparation and are generally faster to cook, making them excellent options.

VEGETARIAN RECIPES

~~~~~~

Indian cuisine naturally lends itself to vegetarian and vegan diets, with many dishes already being plant-based. As such, most of the recipes in this book are suitable for a variety of dietary preferences.

While certain proteins or fats are used in the recipes based on tradition or my personal choice, I encourage you to adapt the dishes to suit your own tastes, budget or available ingredients.

VEGAN RECIPES

〜〜〜〜

The use of vegan yoghurt and other dairy substitutes will transform many of the recipes in this book into vegan-suitable fare. Sometimes all you need to change is the choice of protein. For ease of reference, however, here is list of recipes that are naturally vegan.

MAKE-AHEAD HEROES

Indian food is perfect for batch cooking or preparing ahead of time, making life easier. Curries, especially those made with lentils or meat, often taste even better the next day as the flavours deepen and intermingle. While I typically prepare vegetables, fish and quick stir-fries fresh, or just a few hours in advance, I almost always cook curries in large batches – perfect for unexpected guests or to freeze for a later meal. I believe that if you're investing the time in slow-cooked dishes, it's more practical and energy efficient to make larger quantities and store some for future use.

Beyond curries and dals, breads like fulkas, kokis, naans, theplas, and parathas also freeze well. At home, we separate each bread with a small piece of baking parchment, stack them neatly, then wrap them tightly in a ziplock bag, freezing just enough for two-person meals. These can be cooked directly from frozen on a hot pan or defrosted in the fridge before reheating. Avoid using the microwave for reheating, as it tends to make the breads chewy.

INDEX

RECIPE INDEX

A LITTLE BIT ABOUT ME

I was born in Bombay (now Mumbai) and spent the next 21 years of my life there before moving to England. As children, we travelled across India and would always be trying new dishes as we discovered our vast homeland. Whenever we'd ask to travel abroad instead, like our friends, Dad would say, 'I want to show you your own country first. When you travel abroad eventually, you will be ambassadors of India and should know it well.' How right he was about this (and many other things, too).

My grand-uncle (who we lovingly called Tatun) was a huge influence in my culinary leanings. A man of Tamil descent, he was one of the most gifted cooks I ever met. He'd often arrive at our home unannounced and conjure up the most incredible south Indian meals. They featured vegetables we had never seen before and flavours that were rare in our Gujarati household (Gujarat is a west Indian state).

My maternal grandmother was the most loving cook in the family and definitely a feeder. She'd cook both Gujarati delicacies and British scones with the same enthusiasm. She was also way ahead of her time in the kitchen. You'd never imagine the cookery gadgets and apparatus this sweet, delicate, seemingly sheltered lady had accumulated over the years of accompanying her husband, my flamboyant grandfather, on business travel across the globe. I have no doubt whatsoever that I get my passion for food and penchant for hoarding kitchen contraptions from Nani.

I always believed my path would lead me to the fascinating world of food. Despite studying law at university and a brief stint at a law firm in the City, I eventually opened my first restaurant, Hoppers – a Sri Lankan and south Indian restaurant in London's Soho – in 2015, with my wife and her brothers. The queues for dosas and hoppers at that first 40-seat restaurant proved so long that we went on to open two more Hoppers restaurants. Today, all three are thriving and, like my children, take up most of my time and energy, but give me more joy than I could have ever imagined. My first book, *Hoppers: The Cookbook*, hit the shelves in 2022 and has inspired many dinner parties since. Over the past three years, our Hoppers Feeding the Future programme has built three preschools and fed thousands of children across Sri Lanka.

I travel to India as frequently as I do to Sri Lanka, and each visit deepens my love for India, its food, and culture. At home, I cook Indian food more often than any other cuisine, and I've always felt a strong desire to share my passion for my heritage, especially through its cuisine. It therefore felt instinctive and necessary to teach and write more on the subject. I first tested the waters on my Instagram account, @karancooks, and the Indian recipes there proved an instant success. This further fuelled my desire to write about Indian food, and the idea of *Indian 101* became a reality.

I hope this book proves more than just a set of recipes you want to cook all the time. I hope it inspires you to experiment, discover, study and hopefully even visit my glorious motherland, India.

May, 2025

ACKNOWLEDGEMENTS

Although I've done it once before, I'm still completely blown away by the dedication, attention to detail and team work that go into creating a cookbook. What seems like a collection of beautiful recipes and stories is, in reality, the result of months – sometimes years – of deep research, testing and retesting, tireless writing and pains-taking editing. By the time the final dish is photographed and the last edit made, scores of people have poured hours upon hours into every page and detail.

Cookbooks aren't solitary creations of a chef or food writer. They're the product of a committed team – each member bringing their craft, expertise and a shared vision to the table. The impatient me wishes it were a quicker process (so I could write a lot more, more frequently), but as I have been reminded time and again, good books and ideas develop slowly.

So here I am in spring 2025, three years on from when I first imagined Indian 101, writing the final chapter of what I hope will be a truly magnificent and useful book, one that finds a place in many kitchens for years to come. There are still months of work ahead – proofs to pore over, colours to perfect, schedules to navigate and final tweaks to make. And none of this would be possible without my family and the phenomenal team around me, to whom I owe the biggest thanks, from the bottom of my heart.

Jonny and Sabhbh, my agents – thank you for your belief, guidance and for finding the perfect home for this book.

Luke, my dear friend and brilliant designer – you've surpassed yourself. Thank you for your patience and allowing me to steer from the back seat.

Emily, our project editor – thank you for keeping everything and everyone aligned, and for bringing your sharp insight and expertise at every stage.

Ola and Martina, the ace photography duo – you absolutely nailed the look and feel I was after. Thank you for bringing brightness, energy and love to every image.

Tamara, the magician – I don't know how you made everything look (and taste!) better, with a wave of your spatula. You'd give most seasoned Indian cooks a run for their money. You've been such an inspiration to work with.

Lizzy – thank you for your trust and for championing my vision of Indian 101. I couldn't have asked for a better captain for our ship. And Martha and Annie – for your sharp edits and forensic attention to detail.

Dawn, and the wider sales and PR team – thank you for pushing this book out into the world with such energy, and for listening to and entertaining all my wild PR and social media ideas.

Sarah – simply the best in the book PR business. Thank you for your generosity of praise, humility and unwavering support.

Dasun, Renjith and Haitham – thank you for being my pillars of support at and outside Hoppers, for cheering me on and for sailing the ship while I was buried in this book.

Sukhith, Raashmi and Jack – my tiny but mighty social media team – thank you for taking my vision and bringing it to life with creativity, consistency and patience.

Mum, Dad, Ma, Pa and NP – thank you for everything I am. And both mums especially for your company and advice in the kitchen over the years.

Sunaina, Ayaan and Ishaan – thank you for your patience, for enduring my rollercoaster moods, for grounding me and, vitally, for loving me through the madness of it all.

Jamie, Yotam, Angela and Tom – for your glowing testimonials and support over the years. I'm so grateful.

All my social media and real-world friends, followers and supporters, and those who provided quiet offline support along the way – this book is a result of your encouragement and feedback.

And finally … This, my first Indian cookbook, is for Tatun and Nani. I love and miss you every minute in the kitchen and out of it.